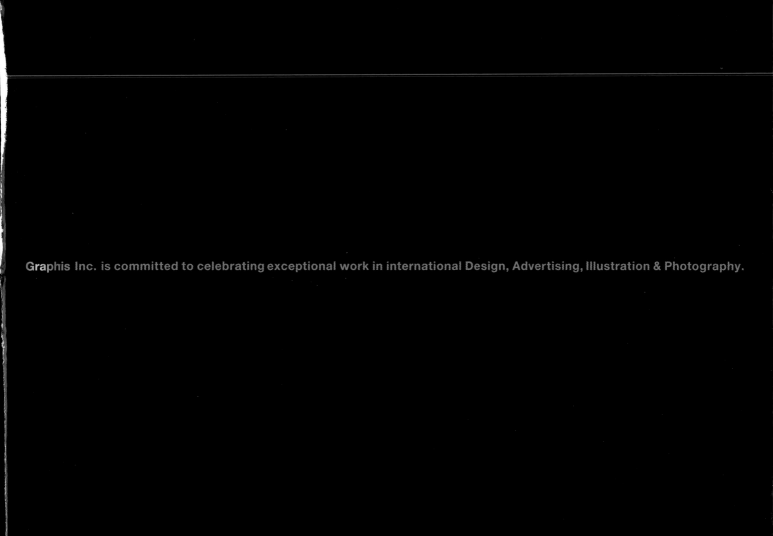

Graphis Inc. is committed to celebrating exceptional work in international Design, Advertising, Illustration & Photography.

Graphis Design Annual 2015

Published by **Graphis** | Publisher & Creative Director: **B. Martin Pedersen** | Executive Director: **Perry Betts** | Designer: **Hee Ra Kim**
Supporting Designer: **Piera Wolf** | Editor: **Rachel Lowry** | Assistant Editor: **Matt Castello** | Production: **Tiffany Washington**

We extend our heartfelt thanks to the contributors internationally who have made it possible to publish a wide spectrum of the best work in Design, Advertising and Photography. Graphis is located at 389 Fifth Avenue, Suite 1105, New York, NY 10016. Anyone is welcome to submit work at www.graphis.com.

Contents

In Memoriam...................................6
Graphis Design Masters Feature............8
Platinum Awards..............................16
Platinum & Gold & Silver Awards...........19
Annual Reports...............................20
Awards.......................................26
Books..28
Branding.....................................38
Brochures....................................67

Calendars....................................78
Catalogs.....................................85
Corporate....................................90
Editorial....................................92
Environmental...............................117
Exhibit.....................................134
Illustration................................139
Interactive Design..........................144
Invitation..................................147

Letterhead..................................148
Logo..150
Outdoor.....................................161
Packaging...................................162
Poster......................................192
Product.....................................210
Promotion...................................213
Restaurant..................................228
Stamps......................................234

Typography..................................235
Credits & Commentary........................237
Index.......................................248
Winners Directory...........................250
Winners by Country..........................252
All Entrants................................253
Graphis Advertisements......................255

Opposite page: "Tulipia #4," photographed by joSon, www.josonsudio.com

Americas

Niels Diffrient
1928-2013
Industrial Designer

Lucia Eames
1930-2014
Designer

Alvin Eisenman
1921-2013
Graphic Designer

Arturo Vega
1947-2013
Designer

Kim Merker
1932-2013
Designer

Charles Pollock
1930-2013
Industrial Designer

Betty Sherrill
1923-2014
Designer

Massimo Vignelli
1931-2014
Designer

A.J. Watson
1924-2014
Car Designer

Asia

John Chun
1929-2013
Designer and Engineer

Pharuephon Mukdasanit
1978-2013
Graphic Designer

Europe

David Collins
1955-2014
Designer and Architect

H.R. Giger
1940-2014
Designer

John Heskett
1937-201
Design professor

Wally Olins
1930-2014
Branding Designer

William Plunkett
1928-2013
Designer

Andrée Putman
1925-2013
Product Designer

Storm Thorgerson
1944-2013
Graphic Designer

Massimo Vignelli
1931-2014
Designer

John Wright
1931-2013
Designer

Opposite page: "Tulipia #4," photographed by joSon, www.josonsudio.com | Following page: "Infiniti," designed by Takenobu Igarashi and photographed by Dale Berman

Alan Fletcher
United Kingdom, *www.graphis.com/bio/alan-fletcher/*

Takenobu Igarashi
Japan, *www.graphis.com/bio/takenobu-igarashi/*

Werner Jeker
Switzerland, *www.graphis.com/bio/werner-jeker/*

João Machado
Portugal, *www.graphis.com/bio/joc3a3o-machado/*

Gunter Rambow
Germany, *www.graphis.com/bio/gunter-rambow/*

Massimo Vignelli

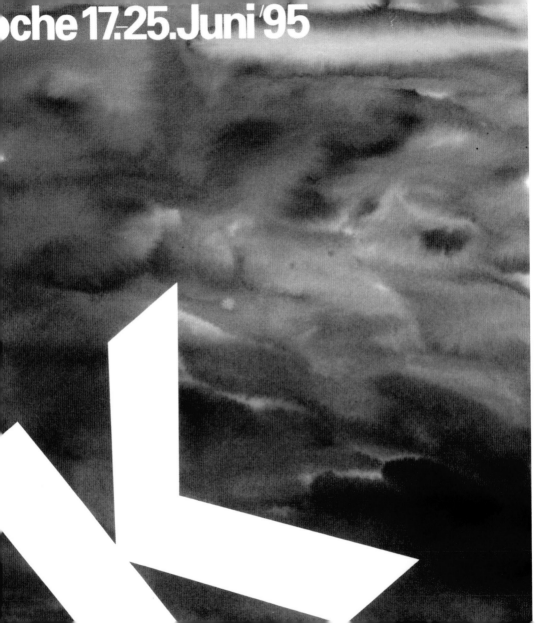

oche 17.–25. Juni '95

Kunsthaus
Zürich

12. März bis
23. Mai 1988

Schweizerische
Stiftung für
die Photographie

Photographien
Filme
Frühe Objekte

M A N

R A Y

EXPODOURO

DESIGN JOÃO MACHADO

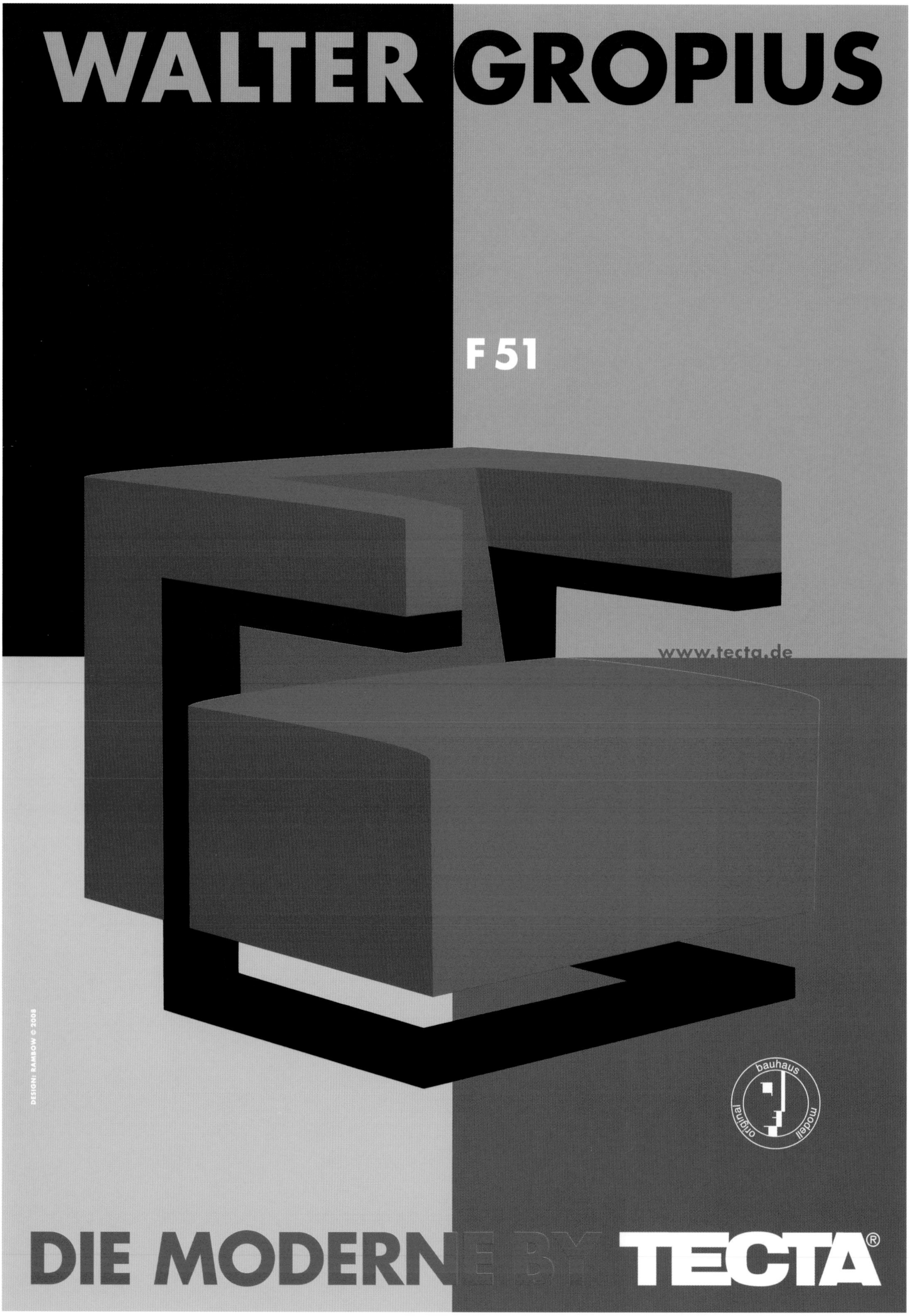

Gunter Rambow | Walter Gropius F51, TECTA | www.gunter-rambow.com

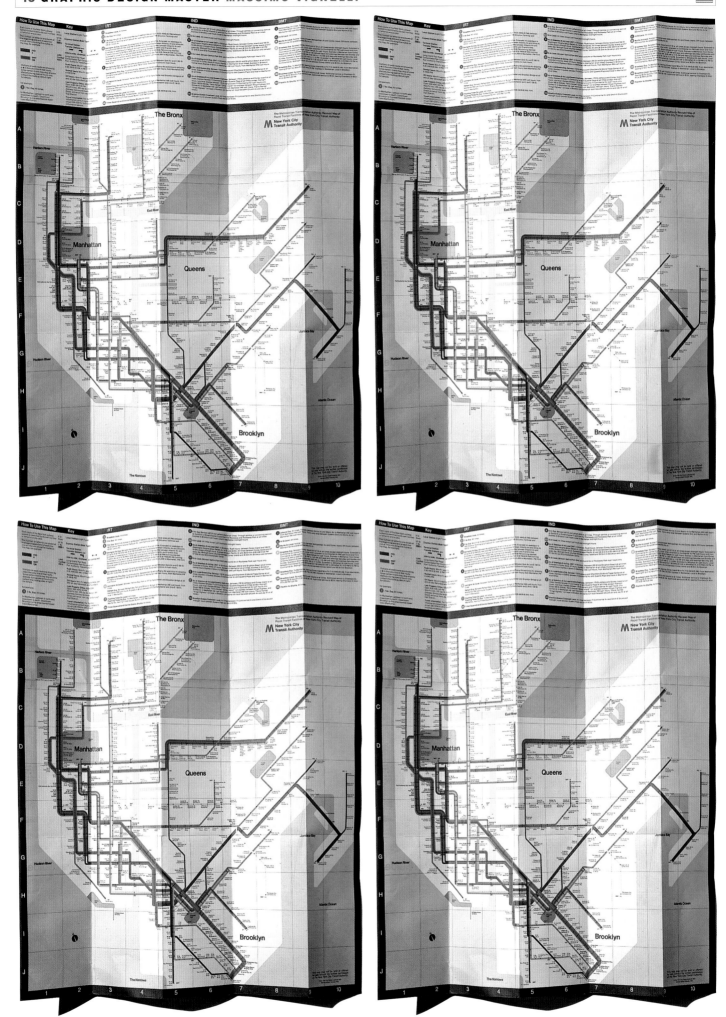

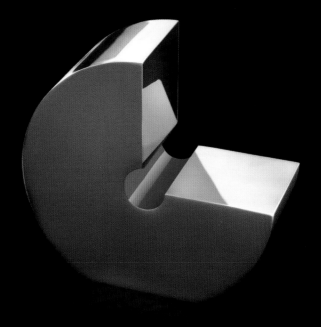

Design Firm: **Rebecca Bartlett LLC** | Client: **Wednesday Seven** | Pages: **228, 229**

Design Firm: **beierarbeit** | Client: **Finanz Informatik** | Page: **184**

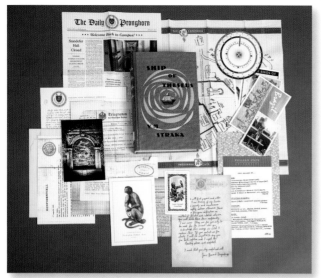

Design Firm: **Headcase Design** | Client: **Melcher Media / Mulholland Books / Bad Robot** | Pages: **28, 29**

Design Firm: **Faith** | Client: **fshnunlimited magazine** | Pages: **104-106**

Design Firm: **Graham Hanson Design**
Client: **Google New York** | Page: **152**

Design Firm: **Frost* Design**
Client: **City Of Sydney** | Pages: **195,196**

Design Firm: **Jan Sabach Design**
Client: **Self initiated, American Red Cross** | Page: **192**

Design Firm: **peter bankov**
Client: **Teatr-Teatr theatrical center in Perm** | Page: **199**

Design Firm: **IF Studio**
Client: **DHA Capital and Continental Properties, Cantor & Pecorella, Inc.** | Pages: **68, 69**

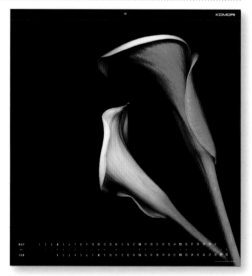

Design Firm: **Toppan Printing Co., Ld.**
Client: **Komori Corporation** | Pages: **79, 80**

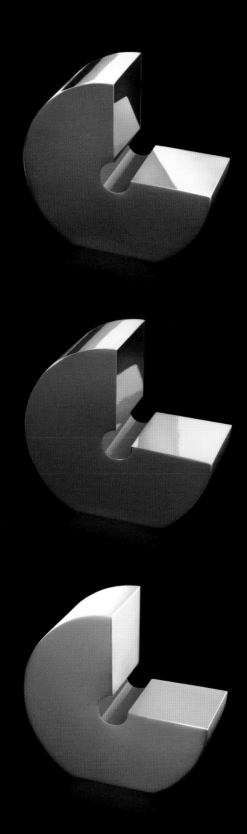

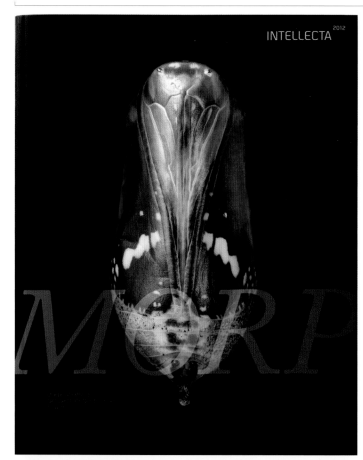

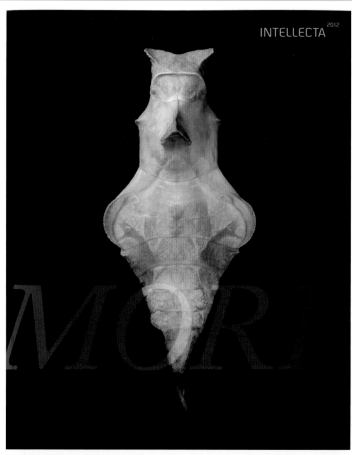

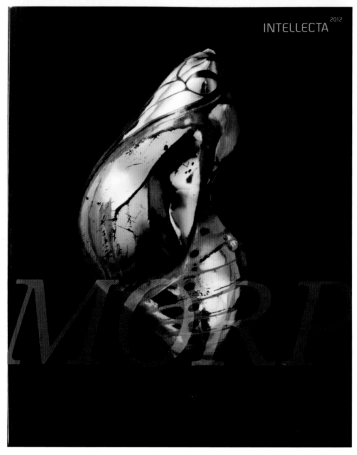

MO RP

INTELLECTA ÄR EN AV SVERIGES STÖRSTA KOMMUNI-
KATIONSKONCERNER, MED FLERA BOLAG PÅ FLERA
ORTER, OCH VERKSAMHETER ÄVEN I DANMARK OCH
KINA. DÄRFÖR HAR VI LAGT STOR VIKT VID ATT HITTA
EN SOLID GEMENSAM VÄRDEGRUND, OCH ATT
ALLTID ARBETA VÄRDERINGSSTYRT.

Fig. 10

**Prognostiserade marknadsföringsinvesteringar
i print resp. online över fem år**

*Analysföretaget Gartner har visat
att MARKNADSCHEFENS
IT-BUDGET INOM FEM ÅR
KOMMER ATT VARA
STÖRRE ÄN IT-CHEFENS.*

Fig. 11

**Vilka aktiviteter har du använt din smartphone
resp. surfplatta till när du läser en tryckt tidning?**

	Smartphone	Surfplatta
Surfat på nätet	54	73
Kommunicerat på nätet	54	59
Sociala medier	53	63
Shoppat	49	63
Dela det jag läst	48	61
Lyssnat på musik	47	79
Sökt lokal info	40	49
Tittat på video	36	47
Familjeaktiviteter	37	44
Arbetat	37	47

processer i bolagen. Möjligheten till samarbete och sam-
verkan ökar och värdeskapandet gynnas.

Digitalt är strategi

Analysföretaget Gartner har visat att marknadschefens
IT-budget inom fem år kommer att vara större än IT-chefens. Digitaliseringen aktualiserar kommunikation som
strategiskt verktyg och digitala strategier kommer allt tyd-
ligare integreras i övergripande företagsstrategier.

Konsumenter och deras varumärken

Förändrade konsumentbeteenden förändrar förutsätt-
ningarna för varumärken. Undersökningar som gjorts

efter finanskrisen visar att starka varumärken klarar sig
betydligt mycket bättre i lågkonjunkturer än mindre kända
varumärken. Samtidigt indikerar flera studier att det finns
ett negativt samband mellan konsumenters starkare röst
och förtroendet för varumärken.

Konsumentrevolutionen har gjort konsumenter i
västvärlden mer ifrågasättande, och högre krav ställs på
företag, inte minst i sociala och miljörelaterade samman-
hang. En studie från Havas visar att endast åtta procent av
européerna och fem procent av invånarna i USA tycker att
varumärken har en positiv inverkan på deras liv. De jäm-
förbara siffrorna för Kina och Latinamerika är 57 respek-
tive 30 procent.

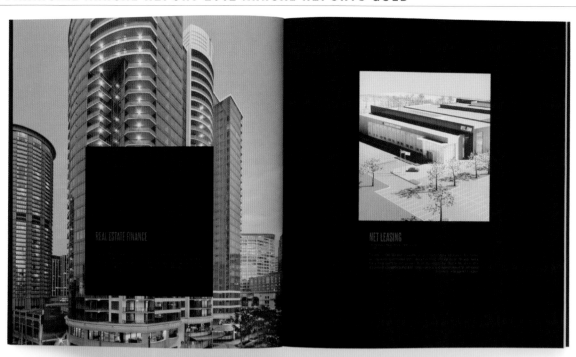

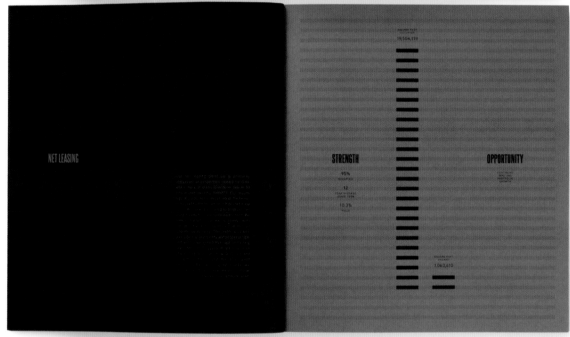

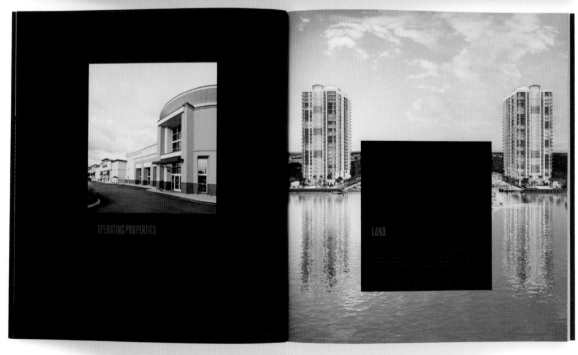

CREATING VALUE

We are focused on creating value for all our stakeholders. From providing world class solutions for our customers, to using our cash flow to de-lever and invest in our operations, we are constantly striving to create value. 2013 will be a year where we continue to deliver for our customers every day in the areas of accountability, service and performance while at the same time we will look to unlock value for our shareholders.

100,000
BUSINESS CARDS
FROM CUSTOMERS

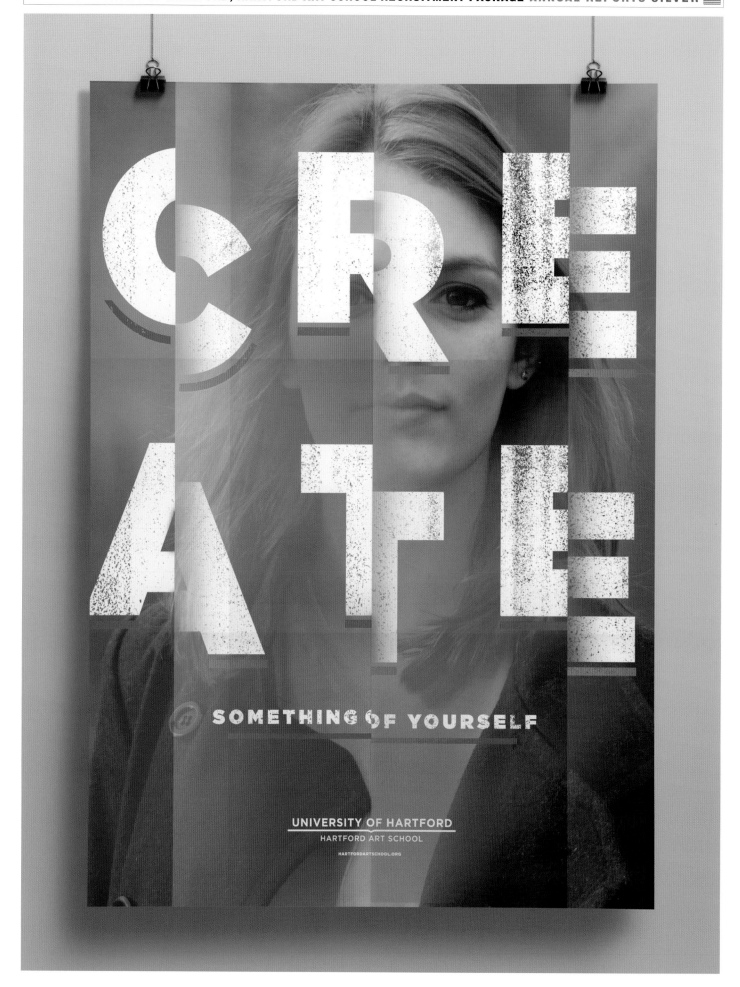

Creating art takes time. So does creating an artist.

NO ONE CAN MAKE YOU AN ARTIST

THAT IS UP TO YOU.

UNIVERSITY OF HARTFORD
HARTFORD ART SCHOOL

hartfordartschool.org

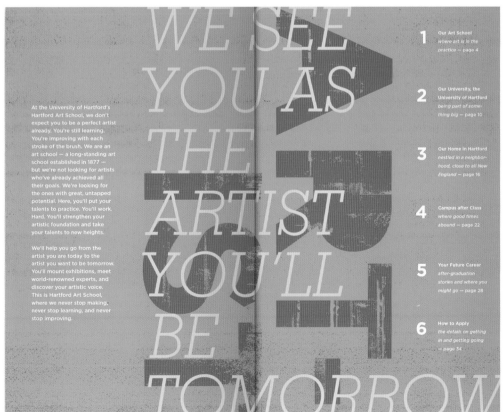

WE SEE YOU AS THE ARTIST YOU'LL BE TOMORROW

At the University of Hartford's Hartford Art School, we don't expect you to be a perfect artist already. You're still learning. You're improving with each stroke of the brush. We are an art school — a long-standing art school established in 1877 — but we're not looking for artists who've already achieved all their goals. We're looking for the ones with great, untapped potential. Here, you'll put your talents to practice. You'll work. Hard. You'll strengthen your artistic foundation and take your talents to new heights.

We'll help you go from the artist you are today to the artist you want to be tomorrow. You'll mount exhibitions, meet world-renowned experts, and discover your artistic voice. This is Hartford Art School, where we never stop making, never stop learning, and never stop improving.

1 Our Art School
where art is in the practice — page 4

2 Our University, the University of Hartford
being part of something big — page 10

3 Our Home in Hartford
nestled in a neighborhood, close to all New England — page 16

4 Campus after Class
where good times abound — page 22

5 Your Future Career
after-graduation stories and where you might go — page 28

6 How to Apply
the details on getting in and getting going — page 34

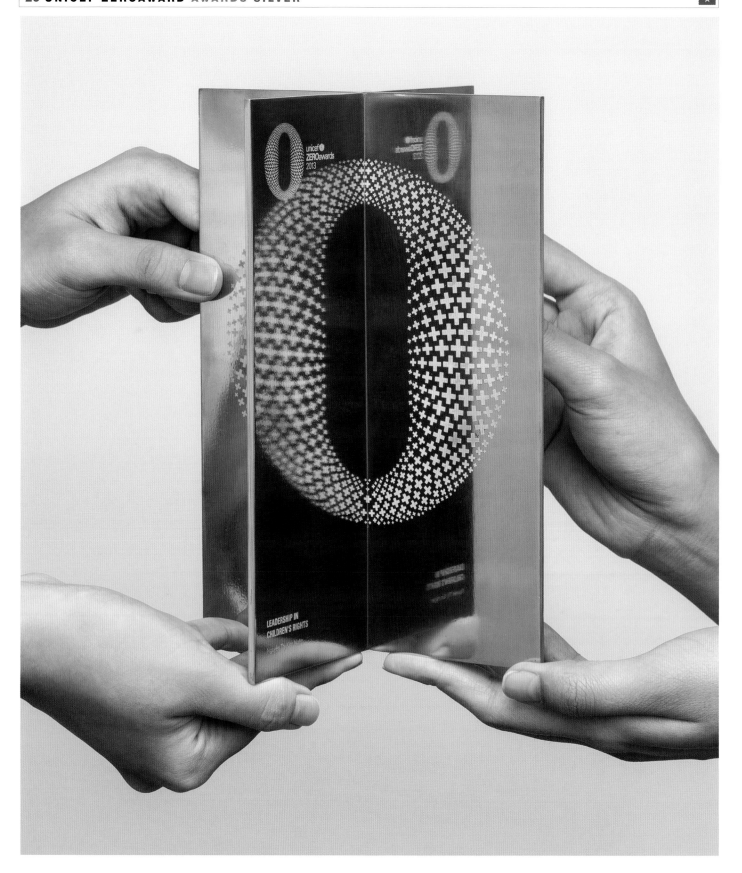

Nuno Duarte Martins | Portuguese Football Federation

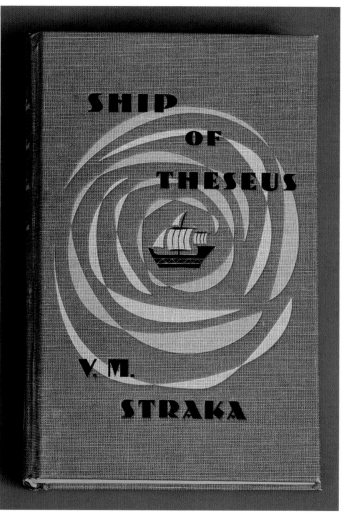

Headcase Design | Melcher Media / Mulholland Books / Bad Robot

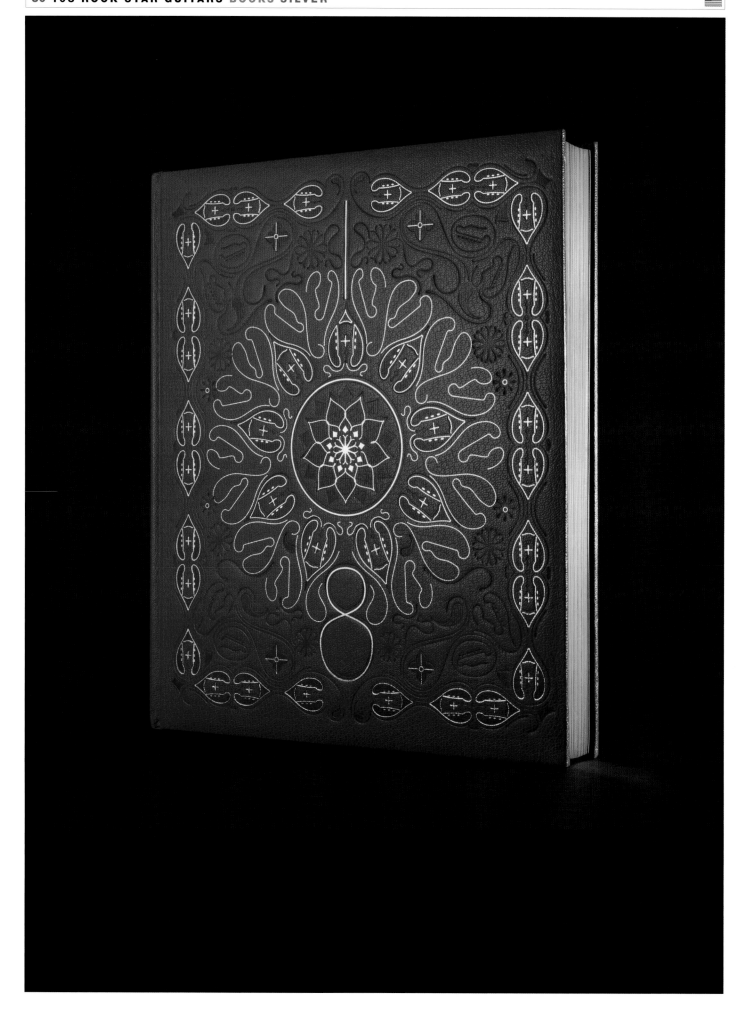

SMOG Design, Inc. | Lisa S. Johnson

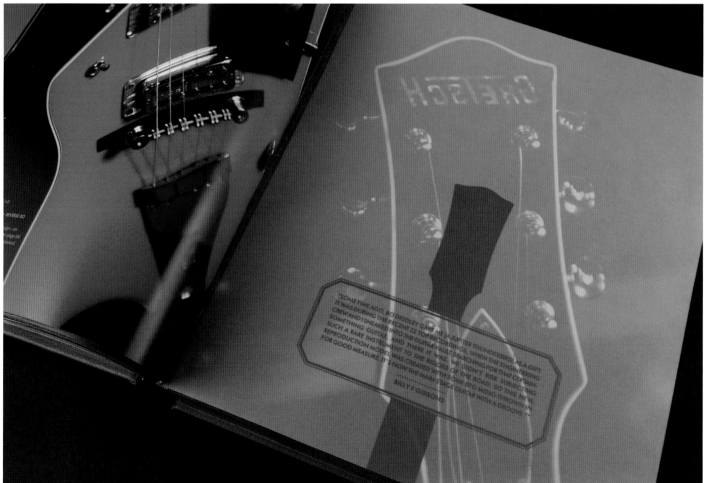

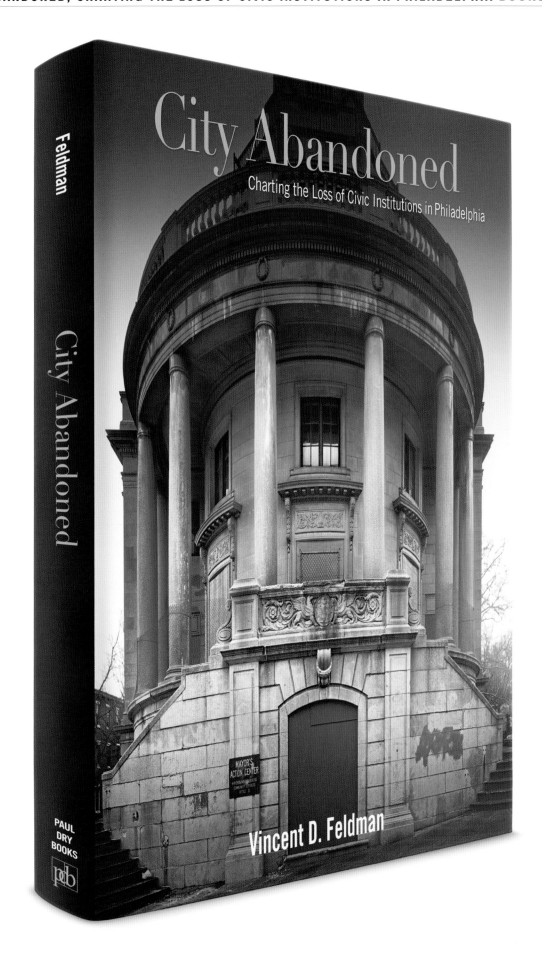

Ohio House, 2005

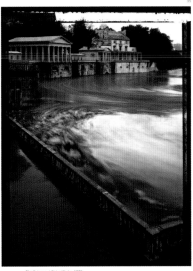

The Fairmount Water Works, 1996

Government

Germantown Hall, 1997

USS Des Moines CA-134, 2005

SS United States, 2006

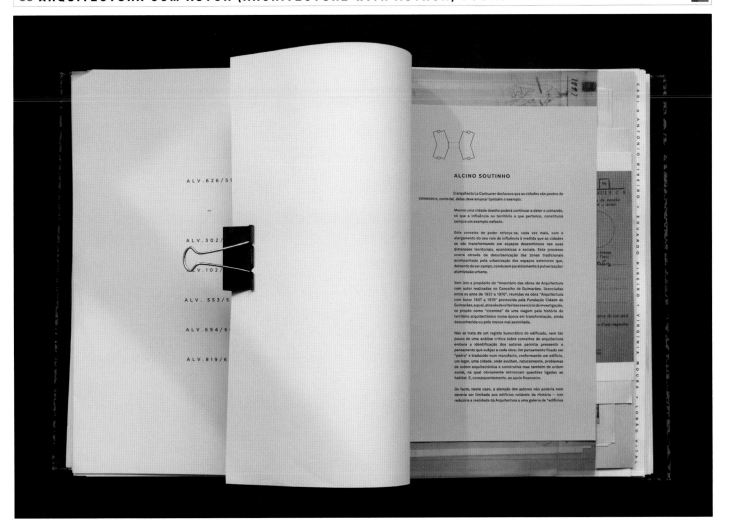

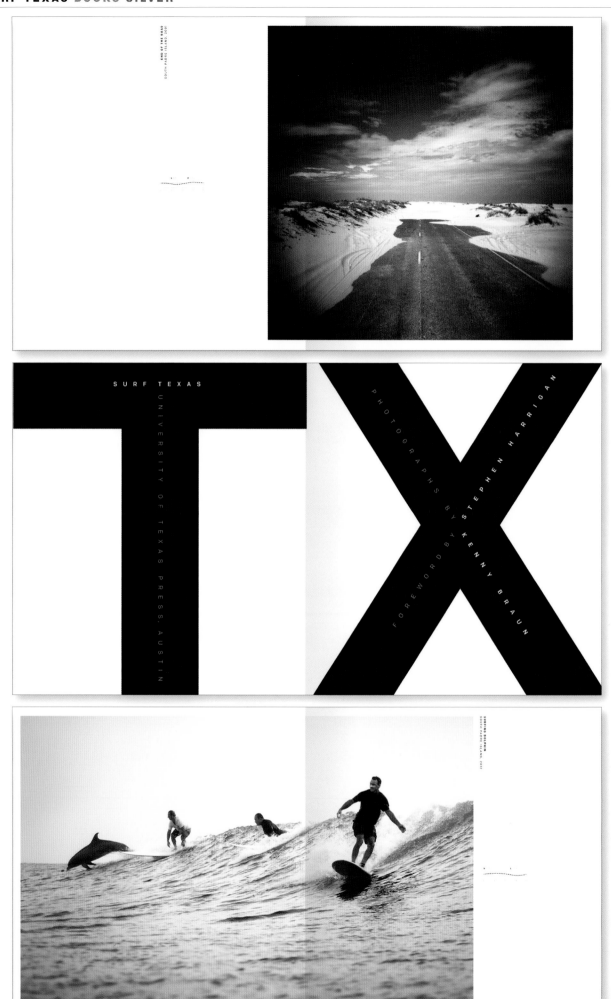

CHECKERED BOARD
SOUTH PADRE ISLAND, 2003

SURFER GIRL
SOUTH PADRE ISLAND, 2007

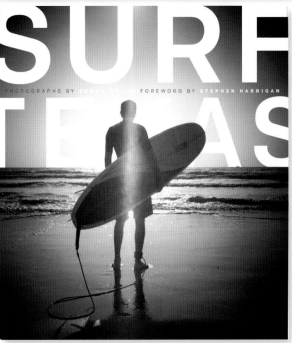

SURF
TEXAS

PHOTOGRAPHS BY KENNY BRAUN   FOREWORD BY STEPHEN HARRIGAN

SURFER'S GARAGE,
SOUTH PADRE ISLAND, 2007

UNDER CURRENTS

I grew up in Houston, about fifty miles from the Gulf Coast. My earliest memories of the beach were of family outings and fishing trips to Rockport with my aunt and uncle. I've always loved being on the Texas coast. But when I discovered surfing, that love turned into an obsession.

No one would confuse the surf in Texas with some famous break on the Pacific Ocean, but that doesn't matter. Texas surfers are as maniacally devoted to the sport as surfers are all over the planet. My friends and I weren't proud; we would surf on anything rideable. We'd drive down to the beach with $30 in our pockets and stay for a week, sleeping in tents and eating sandy sandwiches.

We started riding waves in the mid-seventies, which put us in the second generation of Texas surfers. The first generation consisted of the pioneers from the sixties who discovered surfing in California, wondered whether it could be done in Texas, and brought back boards to give it a try. Texas is not widely known for its great surf but, as that first generation discovered, if you know when to look, and if you look hard and patiently enough, it's there. There are, after all, over 600 miles of coastline, and the Gulf of Mexico reliably produces lots of wind and waves via low pressure systems, northers, storms, and hurricanes.

When I moved to Austin in the mid-eighties and no longer had close access to saltwater, my opportunities for surfing naturally diminished, but my obsession never quite disappeared. I started work on this book twelve years later, in part so that I could reconnect and try to understand what it was about surfing and the Gulf Coast that had made such a deep and permanent impression on me.

I think of myself less as a surf photographer than as a photographer who loves to surf. The essence of surfing, like most sports, is ultimately impossible to photograph or write about. Dreams and memories inform much of the work here. The photographs, I hope, chronicle both Texas's surfing past and its present. At the beach nothing ever changes and nothing is ever the same. The same is true of surfing. Board designs and fashions may change, but the urge to ride a wave, the search for that next perfect swell, is a timeless human preoccupation.

I think about time as I watch the waves growing into the same forms that were seen by our ancient ancestors. As I watch my kids play in the surf, I remember seeing the Gulf for the first time. I remember countless hours spent with friends and family. Time spent at the beach is a return to the source—an intimate and immediate connection with the natural world. You're riding a wave and you look around at the fish and dolphins that are riding it too—and somehow it just makes sense. Surfing has become commercialized, trivialized, and mythologized, but its primal appeal is pure. In these photographs, I hope I have managed to portray some of that enduring fascination, as well as the singular and sometimes unexpected beauty of the Texas coast.

Pentagram | Kenny Braun/University of Texas Press

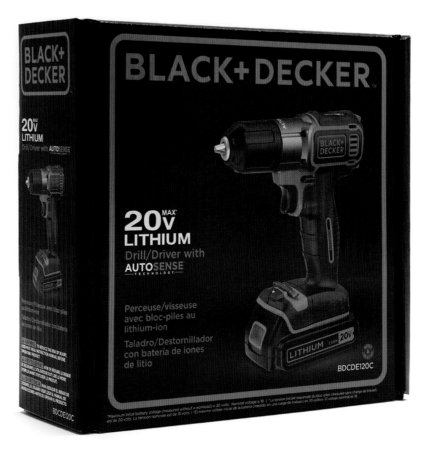

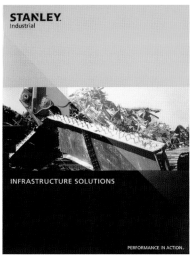

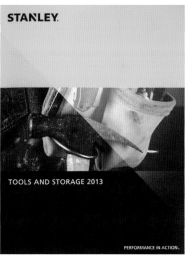

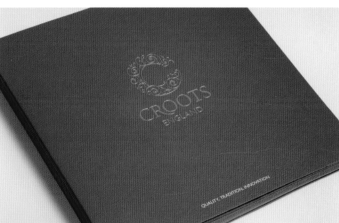

Expanding cinema since 1988
April 10–19, 2014
imagesfestival.com

 Canada Council Conseil des Arts
for the Arts du Canada

 Canadian Patrimoine
Heritage canadien

ONTARIO ARTS COUNCIL
CONSEIL DES ARTS DE L'ONTARIO

TORONTO
ARTS
COUNCIL

TELEFILM
CANADA

The Office of Gilbert Li | Images Festival

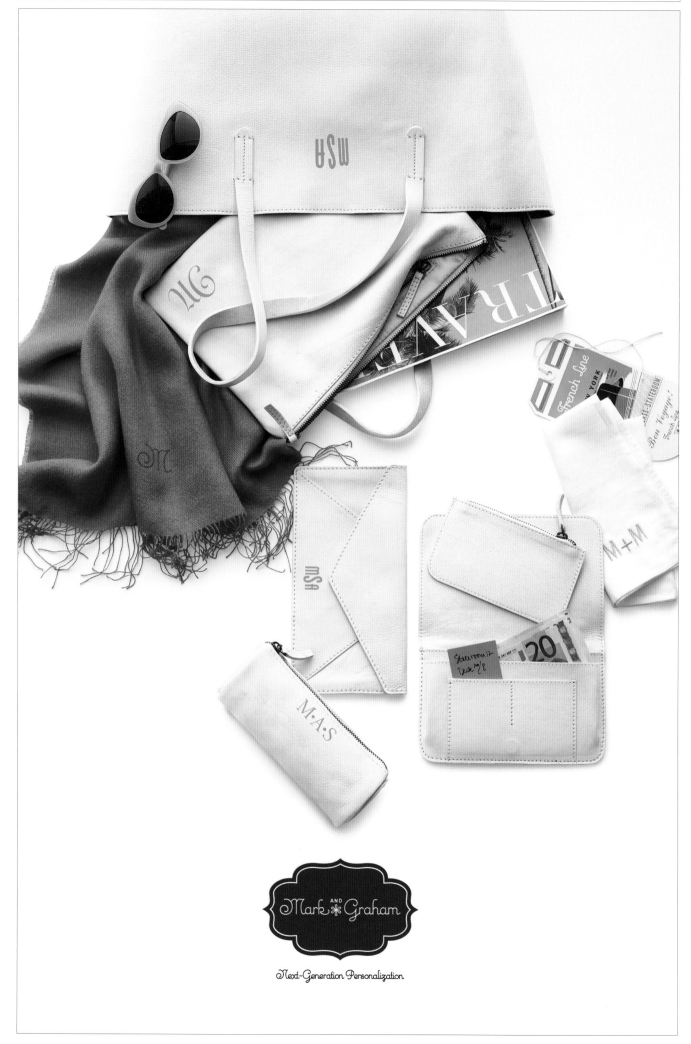

Age is Just a Number

20s, 30s, 40s...
Gifts for every age.

SHOP GIFTS FOR ALL AGES »

Age is Just a Number

20s, 30s, 40s...
Gifts for every age.

SHOP GIFTS FOR ALL AGES »

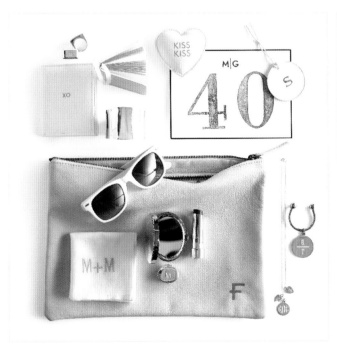

Age is Just a Number

20s, 30s, 40s...
Gifts for every age.

SHOP GIFTS FOR ALL AGES »

Shadia Design | Mark and Joumana Norris

Arcana Academy | Self-Promotion

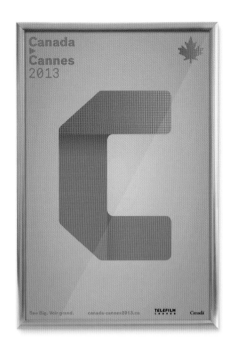

Landor.com

Bangkok
Beijing
Cape Town
Chicago
Cincinnati
Dubai
Geneva
Hamburg
Hanoi
Hong Kong
Jakarta
Kuala Lumpur
London
Melbourne
Mexico City
Milan
Moscow
Mumbai
New York
Paris
San Francisco
Seoul
Shanghai
Singapore
Sydney
Tokyo

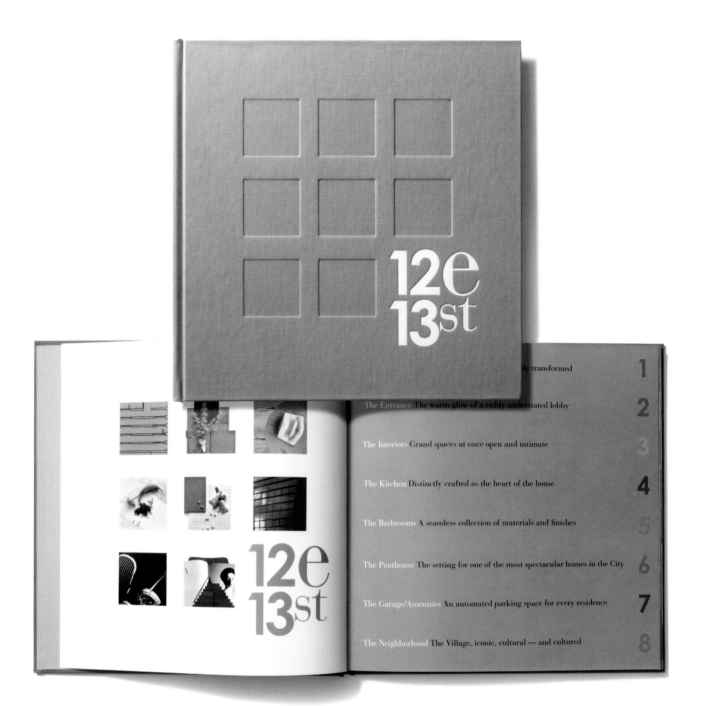

...ly transformed   1

The Entrance **The warm glow of a richly understated lobby**   2

The Interiors Grand spaces at once open and intimate   3

The Kitchen Distinctly crafted as the heart of the home   4

The Bathrooms A seamless collection of materials and finishes   5

The Penthouse The setting for one of the most spectacular homes in the City   6

The Garage/Amenities An automated parking space for every residence   7

The Neighborhood The Village, iconic, cultural — and cultured   8

Powder Room

1

2 Vanity
The powder room vanity cabinet of stained, hand-rubbed East Indian Laurel wood with a base of blackened steel and three-quarter-inch thick honed Kirby Stone countertop adds a rich feel of curated elegance.

3 Floor/Countertop
The floor is tiled in a custom Kirby limestone mosaic of three finishes—honed, flamed and grit-blasted—arranged in a chevron pattern that reflects the signature shapes of the facade, marries with the Kirby Stone countertop.

The Interiors

"There's a serene quality of having every material in your apartment work in unison to create a real environment inside and outside. Details work designed to create a unified whole that is the center of everyone's being. We wanted to make places that would offer people to live their lives and express themselves."

John Cetra, Architect

2 Doors
"The sliding glass walls balance privacy and community. You can be a part of something, and then be separate from everything."

Nancy J. Ruddy, Interior Designer

3 Fixtures/Hardware
White-bronze hardware cast in elemental shapes and forms.

Floor
Inspired by the neighborhood's past wood floors are made of a handsome custom white oak cut in quarter-sawn seven-inch wide planks with a white oil tint finish.

The Garage/Amenities

Private parking at the touch of a button—or your smartphone. Every residence at 12 East 13th Street includes its own automated private parking space, a nod to the building's origin. The state-of-the-art robotic parking system has been designed with the latest technology to automatically park and retrieve your car or SUV from the street-level entrance to the second-floor garage. A fully equipped gym, individual storage units for each residence, and hand-delivered daily mail are also part of the amenities offered.

7

DINOSAUR
DESIGNS

OLSEN ORMANDY

Hoyne | Dinosaur Designs

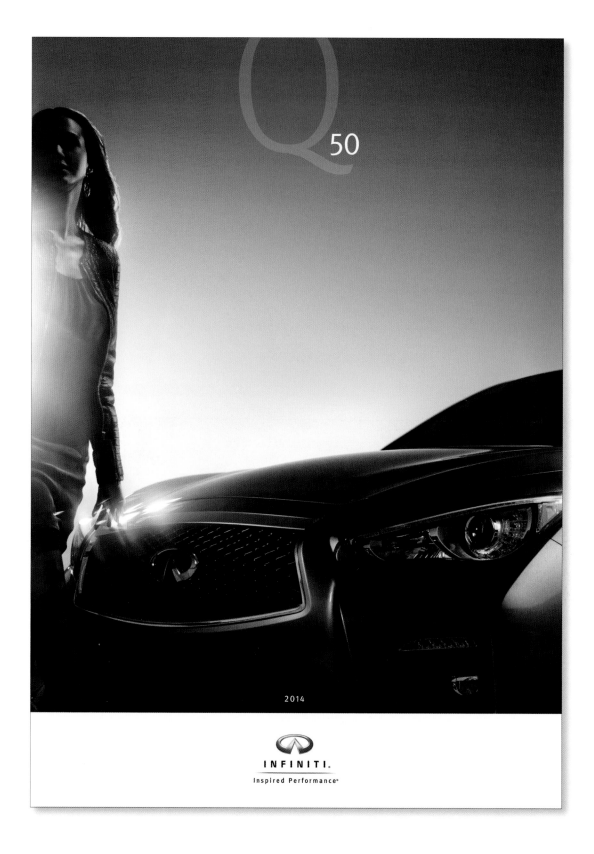

IN MOMENTS

OBJECT OF ATTRACTION
THE ALL-NEW 2014 INFINITI Q50

A JOURNEY

Nine West
Aritzia
Blu's
Banana Republic
Arnold Churgin Shoes
Coach
HS *by* Henry Singer
Melanie Lyne
BCBGMAXAZRIA
Sephora
Brown's Shoes
Michael Kors
J Michaels
Express
RW & Co.

BRAVE & BRIGHT

SOUTHCENTRE

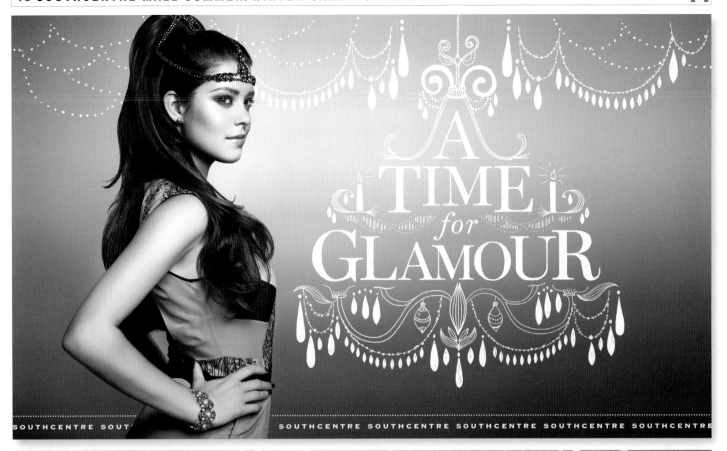

CRAZY ME

81 knotes, 50 metres with a 15 metre transparent sun deck swimming pool, Crazy Me challenges the perception of what a yacht should look like. Heesen custom construction gives each client exactly what they want and Gary Grant's extraordinary exterior design is radically functional. Part of the superstructure retracts to reveal convex windows and a ceiling height of 2.9 metres in the sky lounge. The sound system was created especially for the yacht and integrated into the interior structure. Everything about this yacht is different, even down to the way she was built.

	MPH	KPH	KNOTS
CHAMPION RACEHORSE	40	69	34
HEESEN 65M	33	53	28,8
NUCLEAR SUBMARINE	32	46	28
USAIN BOLT (100M)	27,7	44,7	24,1
DOLPHIN	20	32	17

	HEESEN 65M	AVERAGE 65M DISPLACEMENT YACHT
FULL SPEED	28,8 knots	15 knots
Monaco to Porto Cervo Sardinia	7 hrs 30 mins	15 hrs
Monaco to St Tropez	1 hr 40 mins	3 hrs

CONCLUSION — COMPARED TO THE NEW HEESEN 65 METRE WITH A FAST DISPLACEMENT HULL, THE AVERAGE MOTOR YACHT REQUIRES NEARLY 300 PER CENT MORE POWER TO REACH 15 KNOTS

While other yachts are cruising to the destination, you and your guests are relaxing on the sun deck.

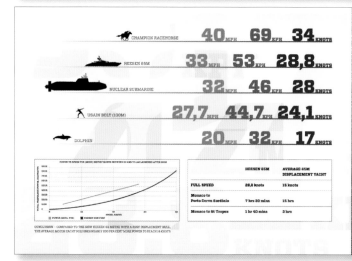

WEIGHT WATCHING

LESS WEIGHT OF A YACHT
INCREASED PERFORMANCE
LESS WEIGHT = INCREASED PERFORMANCE
LESS POWER REQUIRED FOR THE SAME SPEED
LESS FUEL TO CARRY FOR THE SAME RANGE

There are no limits as to how much attention Heesen pays to weight watching. It is one of the most important aspects of how we deliver a virtuous circle of increased performance as well as uncompromised style. Heesen makes things work even when they initially appear impractical. On 50 metre Sky, designer Marx Stumer came up with the idea of solid polished steel blinds to separate the master bedroom and bathroom. Each fin was 8mm thick and the total weight of the blind was over 95 kilos. We took the concept and re-engineered it to look exactly the same except that each fin was 0.75mm thick and the total weight was 12 kilos. Despite reducing the total weight of the yacht by over 7 tonnes, the interior features limestone walls, stainless steel and enormous sheets of thick glass. Heesen has perfected the art of including heavyweight slabs of marble and granite without impacting on the yacht's performance, using a technique that demands tremendous precision, we hone the stone to a thickness of just 4mm. As light as a feather, as strong as steel.

[ambitious]

[expressive]

[swift]

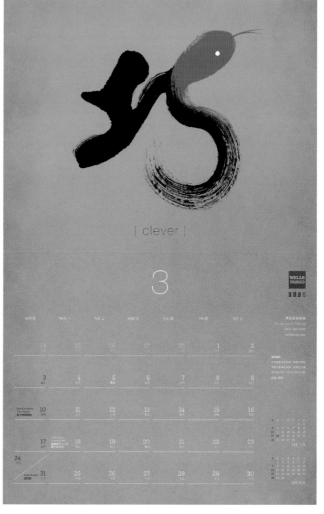

[clever]

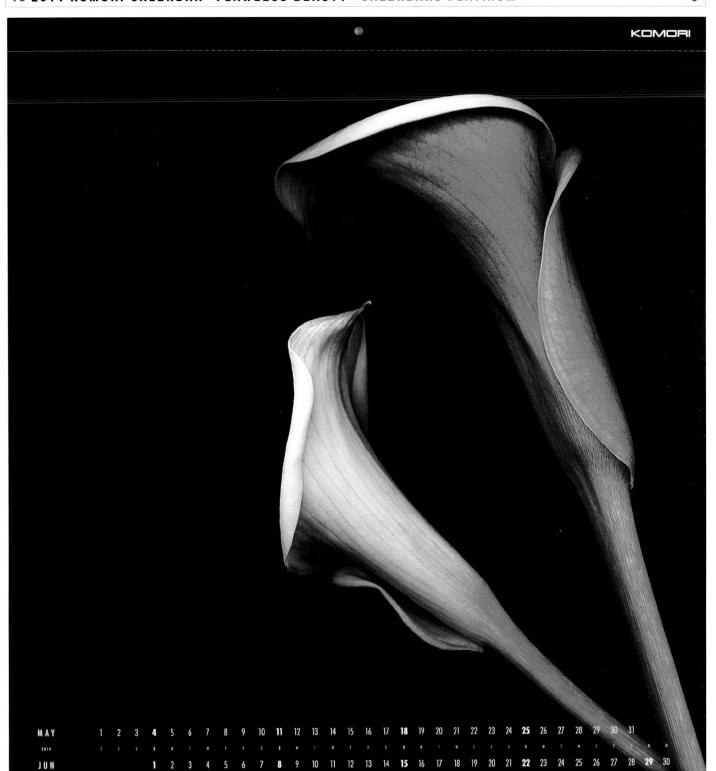

MAY		1	2	3	4	5	6	7	8	9	10	11	12	13	14	15	16	17	18	19	20	21	22	23	24	25	26	27	28	29	30	31
2014		T	F	S	S	M	T	W	T	F	S	S	M	T	W	T	F	S	S	M	T	W	T	F	S	S	M	T	W	T	F	S
JUN			1	2	3	4	5	6	7	8	9	10	11	12	13	14	15	16	17	18	19	20	21	22	23	24	25	26	27	28	29	30

Toppan Printing Co., Ld. | **Komori Corporation**

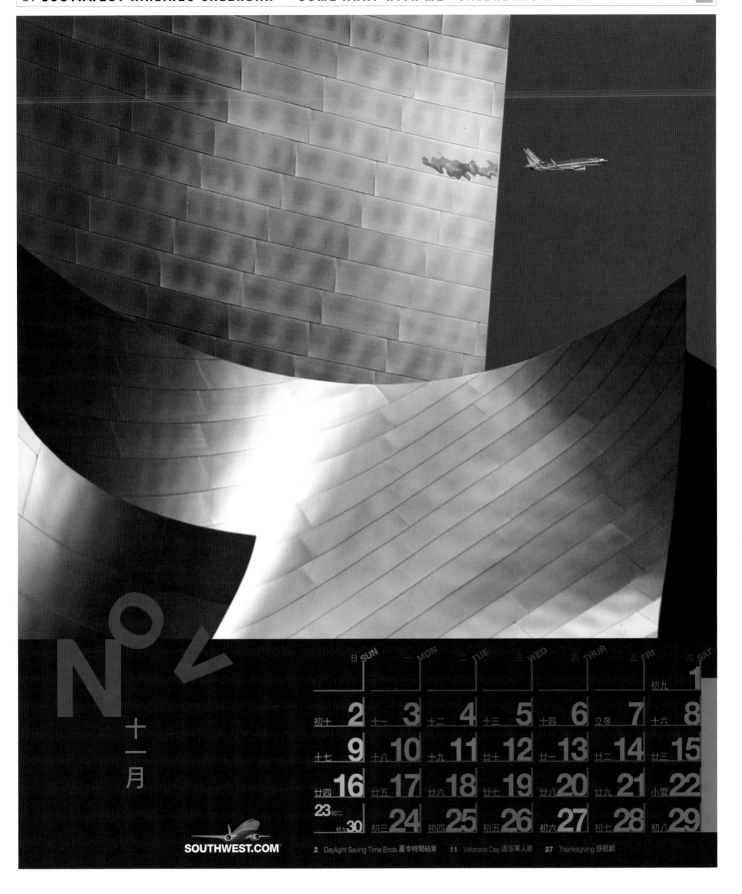

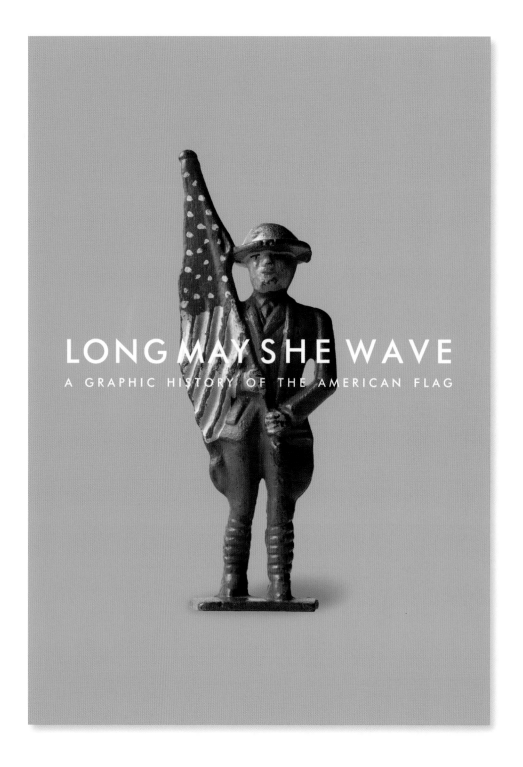

Tin Toy Planes In the 1930s, advances in lithography made it possible to print colorful designs onto tin-plated sheets at 50 sheets per minute, reducing the cost dramatically. These toy planes were manufactured in Japan for the U.S. market.

Children's Toys From the early 20th century, the American flag and patriotic themes were standard images on a wide variety of children's toys, from tin drums and educational games to noisemakers, puzzles and books.

34

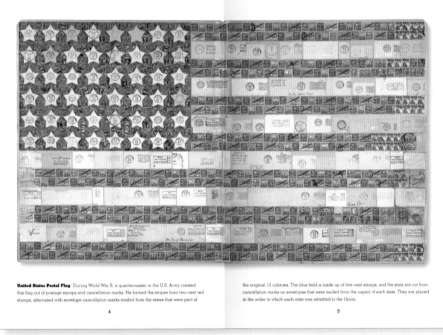

United States Postal Flag During World War II, a quartermaster in the U.S. Army created this flag out of postage stamps and cancellation marks. He formed the stripes from two-cent red stamps, alternated with envelope cancellation marks mailed from the states that were part of

the original 13 colonies. The blue field is made up of five-cent stamps, and the stars are cut from cancellation marks on envelopes that were mailed from the capitol of each state. They are placed in the order in which each state was admitted to the Union.

4

5

Chinese Silk Embroidery The opening of Chinese ports to American trade in the late 19th century prompted Chinese artisans to produce goods that would appeal to the American sailors and merchant marines who called on their ports.

Flag Guitar This patriotic electric guitar is from the Dave Matthews Band. Every member of the band autographed the guitar and donated it for auction to benefit first responders to the 9/11 tragedy.

19

Studio Hinrichs | Stars & Stripes Foundation

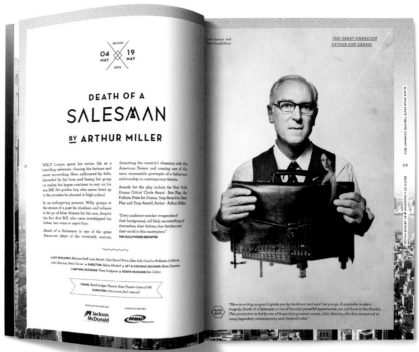

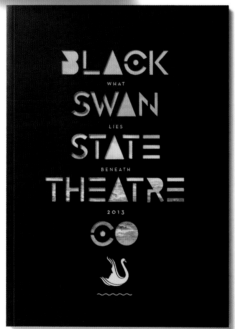

CHAIR RICHARD WILDE

DESIGN

717 students   110 faculty members   149 classes

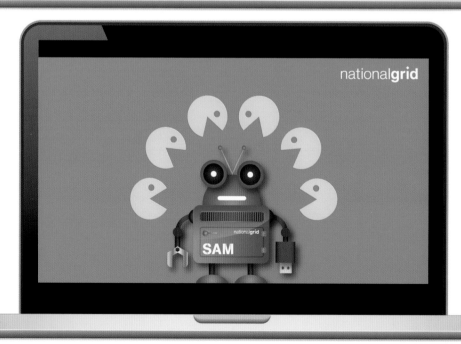

GQ   NOV   2013   P 192

CONFESSIONS OF A DRONE WARRIOR

-147

109

VV 200

HE WAS AN EXPERIMENT, REALLY.
ONE OF THE FIRST RECRUITS FOR A NEW
KIND OF WARFARE IN WHICH MEN AND
MACHINES MERGE. HE FLEW MULTIPLE
MISSIONS, BUT HE NEVER LEFT HIS
COMPUTER. HE HUNTED TOP TERRORISTS,
SAVED LIVES, BUT ALWAYS FROM AFAR.
HE STALKED AND KILLED COUNTLESS
PEOPLE, BUT COULD NOT ALWAYS TELL
YOU PRECISELY WHAT HE WAS HITTING.
MEET THE 21ST-CENTURY AMERICAN
KILLING MACHINE. WHO'S STILL
UTTERLY, TERRIFYINGLY HUMAN

BY Matthew Power

Ethan Levitas

IT WAS A TINY TOWN OF FARMERS, a village where everyone knew everyone and nearly all struggled to make ends meet. But then, a few days before Christmas, they won the largest lottery in the history of Spain. The entire town. All of them.

(Well, almost all of them.) Instantly, SODETO became known as the luckiest place on earth. Michael Paterniti visits the town that fortune smiled upon and finds that the people there—now flush—are still uncertain of just how lucky they really are

Geof Kern

THE Luckiest Village IN THE WORLD

GQ
AUG
'13

PG.
117

THE SWEAR JAR

JAY KIRK was a normal, well-adjusted adult with a massive f#x*ing cursing problem. He cursed in the shower. He cursed in front of his 6-year-old daughter. He cursed at the goddamned sh!t-eating morons at Whole Foods when they ran out of Japanese eggplant. The problem seemed unfixable. That is, until his wife came up with a curious solution that could either cure him, or kill him

Franck Allais

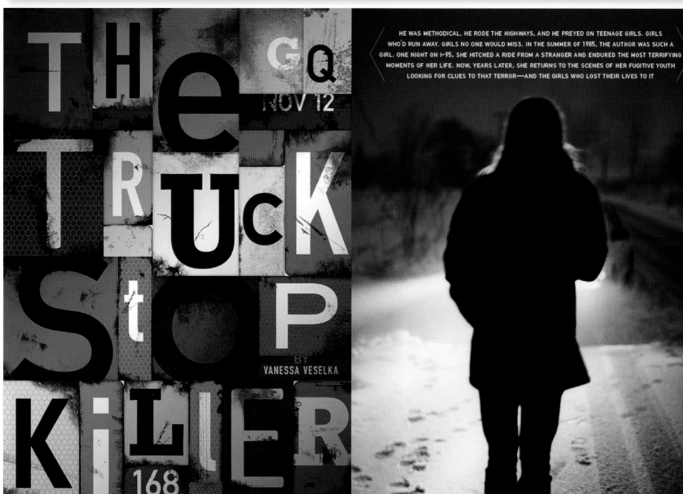

HE WAS METHODICAL, HE RODE THE HIGHWAYS, AND HE PREYED ON TEENAGE GIRLS. GIRLS WHO'D RUN AWAY. GIRLS NO ONE WOULD MISS. IN THE SUMMER OF 1985, THE AUTHOR WAS SUCH A GIRL. ONE NIGHT ON I-95, SHE HITCHED A RIDE FROM A STRANGER AND ENDURED THE MOST TERRIFYING MOMENTS OF HER LIFE. NOW, YEARS LATER, SHE RETURNS TO THE SCENES OF HER FUGITIVE YOUTH LOOKING FOR CLUES TO THAT TERROR—AND THE GIRLS WHO LOST THEIR LIVES TO IT

GQ
NOV 12

THE TRUCK STOP KILLER

BY
VANESSA VESELKA

168

Love
Sex
&
Madness

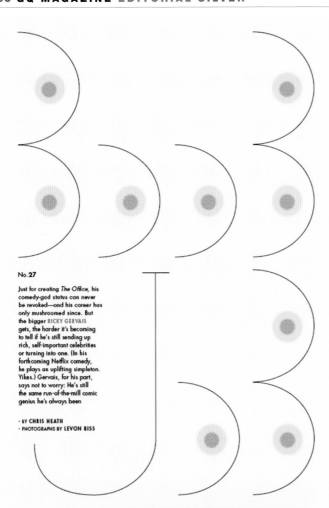

No. 27

Just for creating *The Office*, his comedy-god status can never be revoked—and his career has only mushroomed since. But the bigger RICKY GERVAIS gets, the harder it's becoming to tell if he's still sending up rich, self-important celebrities or turning into one. (In his forthcoming Netflix comedy, he plays an uplifting simpleton. Yikes.) Gervais, for his part, says not to worry: He's still the same run-of-the-mill comic genius he's always been

· BY CHRIS HEATH
· PHOTOGRAPHS BY LEVON BISS

BRAD HARRIS

4TH & FOREVER

>> For every Peyton, Brady, or Brees, there are a hundred NFL hopefuls who don't dream of stardom. They just want a job. They show up at training camp, work their asses off, and pray not to get cut. For these anonymous guys on the NFL bubble,

214 GQ 11.13

every hard knock, every missed tackle, is compounded by the psychic burden of living each practice in limbo. This is the story of three bubble players—a quarterback, a receiver, and a kicker—and their now-or-never gridiron dreams
BY DANIEL RILEY

NATURAL BORN KILLERS

WOMEN GET FLUSTERED UNDER FIRE. THEY'RE TOO FRAGILE, TOO EMOTIONAL. THEY LACK THE FEROCITY REQUIRED TO TAKE A LIFE. THEY CAN'T HANDLE PAIN. THEY'RE A DISTRACTION, A THREAT TO UNIT COHESION, A PROVOCATIVE TEASE TO CLOSE-QUARTERED MEN.

These are the sort of myths you hear from people who oppose the U.S. military's evolving new rules about women in combat. But for the women who have already been in combat, who have earned medals fighting alongside men, the war stories they tell don't sound a thing like the myths

by NATHANIEL PENN ▪▪ Danielle Levitt

98 GQ 2013

Oops, You Just Hired The Wrong

By **Jeanne Marie Laskas**

PHOTOGRAPHS BY
Jonathon Kambouris

SAY YOU WANT SOMEONE, YOU KNOW, **eliminated**—*a lover, a business partner, a mother-in-law.* THERE ARE GUYS OUT THERE WHO WILL DO THAT. FOR A PRICE. THEN THERE'S *another kind of guy.* A GUY WHO LOOKS AND ACTS JUST LIKE **a regular hit man.** PRISON TATS, DO-RAG. BUT INSTEAD OF DOING THE JOB, HE TURNS SIDES, *and then you realize that* YOU WERE HIS TARGET ALL ALONG

11·13
GQ
184

Men OF THE Year 2013

240 GQ/MOTT DECEMBER 2013

CL☁UDY
with a Chance of **Stinging-Nettle Flan** *and* **Tomato Coulis**

HOW DID PORTLAND, A SOGGY CITY ON THE WEST COAST, COME TO BE THE SCRAPPIEST, MOST ORIGINAL GASTRONOMIC DESTINATION IN AMERICA, A TOWN WHERE YOU CAN EAT EVERYTHING FROM FOOD-TRUCK FEASTS TO FOUR-STAR SPREADS THAT RIVAL FANCIER (AND WAY MORE EXPENSIVE) PLACES? *ALAN RICHMAN* EXPLORES THE FOOD WORLD'S NEW PROMISED LAND—AND EXPLAINS WHY YOU SHOULD GO NOW, WHILE THE GOOD TIMES LAST

PEDEN • MUNK

128-GQ11.12

Everyone's a

COMEDIAN

COMEDY USED TO BE A SPECIALTY FIELD

THE SAME WAY OPEN-HEART SURGERY WAS LEFT TO, YOU KNOW, DOCTORS, SO TELLING JOKES AND DOING PRATFALLS WAS LEFT TO THE PROFESSIONALS.

NOW A GOOD ONE-LINER is part of everyone's job description.

DON'T BELIEVE US?

TELL IT TO OSCAR NOMINEE AND DISTINGUISHED THESPIAN JAMES FRANCO, WHO ALSO KNOWS HOW TO MAKE JOKES ABOUT THE APOCALYPSE AND MALE BONDING.

(IT'LL ALL MAKE SENSE IN A FEW PAGES.)

It's not just that every*one* must be funny. Every*thing* must be funny.

LIKE:

BEARDS!

DOG HUMPING!

TAYLOR SWIFT!

ROBOTS!

DEAD MEN!

ENGLISHMEN!

That awkward moment right after sex!

The last few hours before the end of the world!

In honor of GQ's fifth annual—except for that time we skipped a year—comedy issue, we enlisted some of our favorite specialists (RICKY GERVAIS, DANNY McBRIDE, BILL HADER, WILL ARNETT...), plus a few amateurs (the drummer for the Black Keys!),

TO HELP US CELEBRATE THE **40** THINGS MAKING US LAUGH RIGHT NOW

TERRY RICHARDSON

SEA TO LAND
Sporting a homemade mask and trailing his makeshift spear gun, Ishmael Said emerges from the water after an unsuccessful octopus hunt.

Call Them Ishmael

Crafting a new kind of sanctuary along Mozambique's coast

by **Alex MacLennan**
photographs by **James Morgan**
illustrations by **Melinda Josie**

A

AS OUR BOAT BANGS UP to the beach on Ilha de Mafamede through a jostle of bright sky, rushing waves and choppy blue-green water, Ishmael Said is the first to hop out.

At 66, Ishmael is spry and full of energy despite the bumpy hour-long ride. With gray sprigs in his hair, a scraggly beard, and the wiry arms of an athlete, he laughs as we struggle out of the heaving boat into the surf, helping us grab bags and ordering people around with jokes and hearty slaps on the back.

Mafamede is a tiny island, and as we begin to unload our gear, he sparks a playful competition with John Guernier, Primeiras e Segundas program manager for the CARE-WWF Alliance, to see who can lug the most supply tubs the short distance from boat to campsite in the

---

Photographs by **Nine François**

NINE FRANÇOIS has been teaching and practicing photography for more than 20 years from her home base in Austin, Texas. Of taking these wild portraits, François says: "I've learned how to get close, work fast, hold my ground in some cases, and run like hell in others." To see more from her *Animalia* series, visit **ninefrancois.com**.

"CAIMAN"

"ZEBRA"

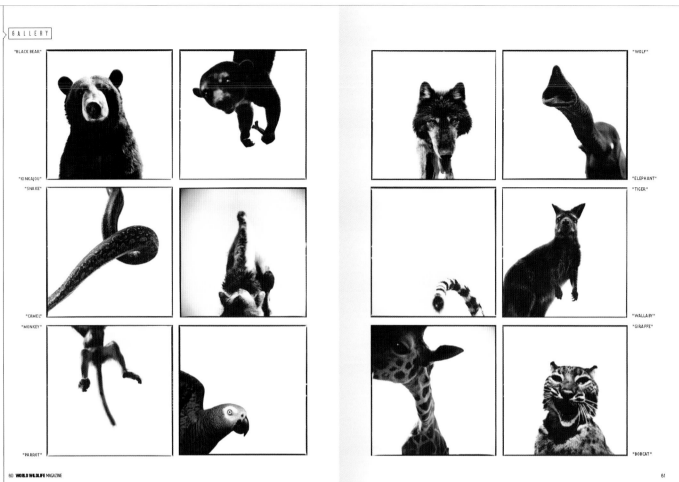

WORLD WILDLIFE

**INCREASINGLY
MODERN MYANMAR**

Take a tour through Myanmar—a country
rich in resources, diverse in culture and
undergoing a blistering rate of change.

42 / WILDLIFE CRIME COMES HOME
50 / DRINK IN A GRAY WHALE'S GAZE

WWF

SPRING
2014

GALLERY

Photographs by **Andrew Zuckerman**

Regular trips to see the famous dioramas in New York City's
Museum of Natural History, paired with a desire to objectively
catalog the natural world, inspired photographer **ANDREW
ZUCKERMAN** to create *Creature*. "What was so interesting about making the project," he says, "was finding a way
to photograph such spontaneous subjects within fairly rigid
self-imposed constraints." Find more striking *Creature*
images at **creaturebook.com**.

GIRAFFE
Giraffa camelopardalis

COMMON WARTHOG
Phacochoerus africanus

GALLERY

BLUE AND YELLOW MACAW
Ara ararauna

SILVER AROWANA
Osteoglossum bicirrhosum

RED KANGAROO
Macropus rufus

GREEN IGUANA
Iguana delicatissima

COMMON CHIMPANZEE
Pan troglodytes

CORN SNAKE
Pantherophis guttatus

60 **WORLD WILDLIFE** MAGAZINE

DISPATCH

MAGDALENA BAY · BAJA CALIFORNIA SUR, MEXICO

ALONG THE WHALES' HIGHWAY
Protecting gray whales in Baja and the Beaufort Sea

How far would you travel for a good meal? Whatever your answer, it's probably not as ambitious as the journey of a gray whale. Each year, gray whales in the eastern Pacific traverse a 6,000-mile course that stretches from winter breeding grounds in the shallow lagoons of Baja, Mexico, to summer feeding grounds in Alaska's frigid Beaufort Sea—one of the longest mammal migrations on the planet. In March 2011, photographer Florian Schulz caught the gaze of one such whale.

In the warm waters off the Baja Peninsula, whales gather for courtship and mating, while already expectant mothers give birth to calves. Here, research teams study whale health and populations, looking for evidence of threats individuals have faced on their journey south, such as ship strike scars or chemical pollution in body tissue. Arctic efforts focus on the whales' feeding grounds, addressing threats posed by oil and gas development and shipping. A WWF-supported research team is also mapping the region's biodiversity, physical features, and likely evolution in the face of climate change—all to identify the most crucial areas for wildlife.

In brief, we're trying to keep these areas safe, so gray whales will face fewer dangers as they swim north for a hard-earned feast.

FASHION UNLIMITED

AUTUMN/WINTER 2013 · ISSUE 1

fshnunlimited

AUTUMN | WINTER
2013
$13.99

33

0 74470 94897 1

THROUGH THE LOOKING GLASS

Resident artist Bruno Billio's apartment at the Gladstone Hotel invites you through the looking glass and into the visionary's head

Photography by Roger Chen

MODE

SIGN
Vicky Lam LAN-
GUAGE

Photographer Vicky Lam's fascination with bright lights and an obsession for colour, elevate the illuminated store fronts of Hong Kong's Canton Road to high art

Photographer Vicky Lam's fascination with bright lights and an obsession for colour, elevate the illuminated store fronts of Hong Kong's Canton Road to high art

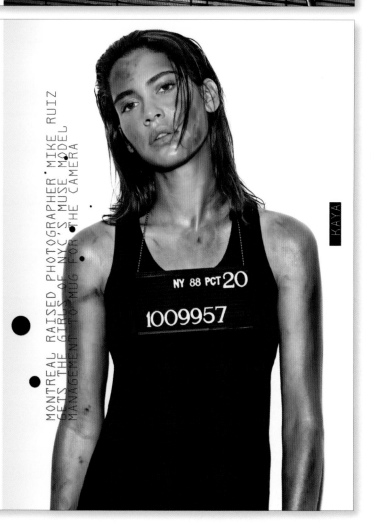

MONTREAL RAISED PHOTOGRAPHER MIKE RUIZ GETS THE GIRLS OF NYC'S MUSE MODEL MANAGEMENT TO MUG FOR THE CAMERA

KAYA

NY 88 PCT 20

1009957

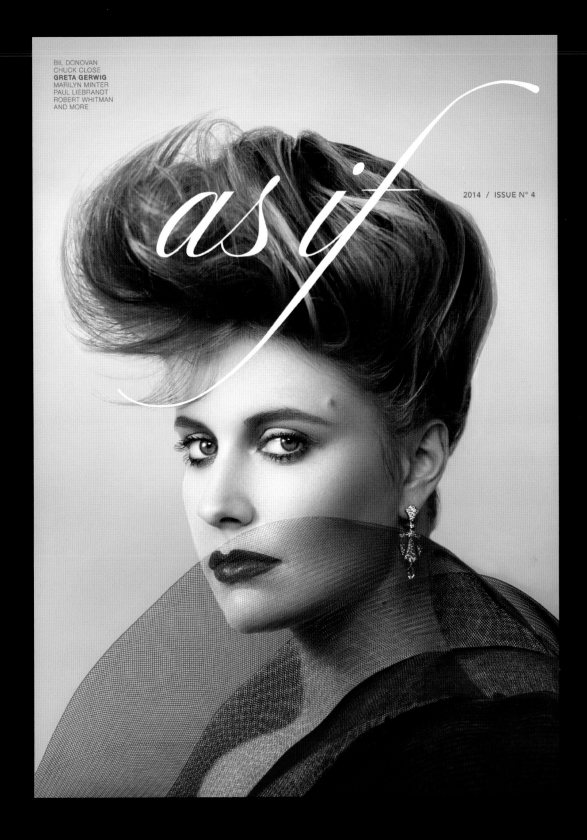

BIL DONOVAN
CHUCK CLOSE
GRETA GERWIG
MARILYN MINTER
PAUL LIEBRANDT
ROBERT WHITMAN
AND MORE

as if

2014 / ISSUE N° 4

AS IF Media Group, LLC | AS IF Magazine

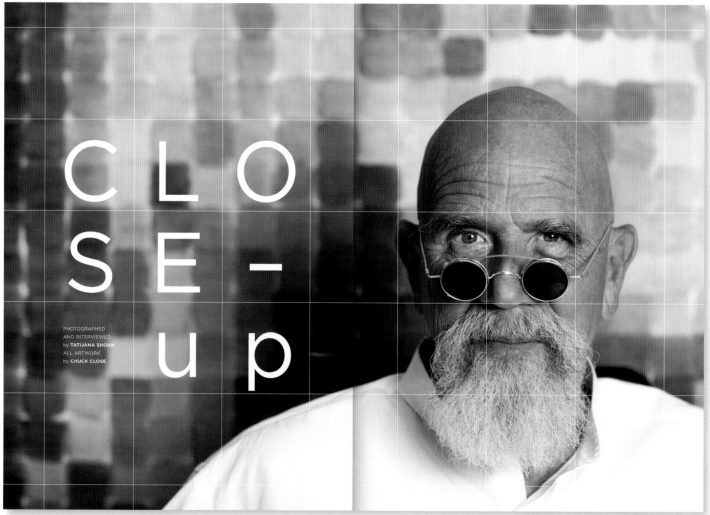

CLO SE- up

PHOTOGRAPHED
AND INTERVIEWED
by **TATIJANA SHOAN**
ALL ARTWORK
by **CHUCK CLOSE**

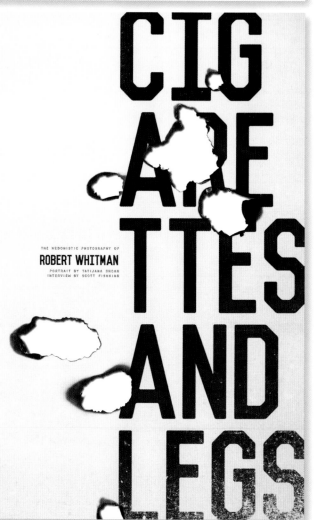

CIG ARE TTES AND LEGS

THE HEDONISTIC PHOTOGRAPHY OF
ROBERT WHITMAN
PORTRAIT BY TATIJANA SHOAN
INTERVIEW BY SCOTT FISHKIND

I FIRST MET ROBERT WHITMAN IN NEW YORK BACK IN 1995. HE IS LIKE HIS PHOTOS: IMAGINATIVE, DYNAMIC, RAW, SURPRISING, AND UNFORGETTABLE. CLOSEUPS OF BODY PARTS IN VARIOUS ENVIRONMENTS AND STATES OF DRESS AND UNDRESS GIVE THE VIEWER A SENSE OF LOOKING THROUGH A PEEPHOLE. WHEN LOOKING AT WHITMAN'S ARCHIVES IT'S NOT SURPRISING THAT HE HAS BEEN AN INSPIRATION FOR MANY PHOTOGRAPHERS WHO TRANSLATE HIS RAW, SPONTANEOUS STYLE INTO HIGHLY PRODUCED SLEAZE-CHIC FASHION SHOOTS. WHITMAN MAY BE THE GRANDFATHER OF SLEAZE-CHIC, BUT HIS HONEST AND DIRECT APPROACH TRANSLATES INTO SENSUAL AND EMOTIONAL PHOTOS OF DANCERS, DYNAMIC AND RICH TRAVEL ESSAYS, AND INTIMATE AND THOUGHTFUL PORTRAITS OF EVERYDAY PEOPLE. WE WERE DELIGHTED WHEN WHITMAN AGREED TO BE OUR SUBJECT IN THIS ISSUE, BUT THE HARD PART CAME WHEN WE HAD TO CHOOSE WHAT PHOTOS WE WANTED TO SHOWCASE. WE LOOKED THROUGH THOUSANDS OF PHOTOS THAT SPANNED DECADES AND DESTINATIONS UNTIL A THEME AROSE THAT WE FOUND PROVOCATIVE: CIGARETTES AND LEGS. HIS FASCINATION FOR THESE TWO SUBJECTS IS EVIDENT. I SAT DOWN WITH MY OLD FRIEND TO TALK ABOUT HOW, WHY, WHERE, AND WHEN IT ALL BEGAN.

WHITMAN 1979 MINNEAPOLIS IMAGE 0305

TWENTY FIRST CENTURY MUSE

PHOTOS BY BERT STERN, COMPLIMENTS OF TASCHEN PUBLISHING

WRITTEN BY PENNY ARCADE

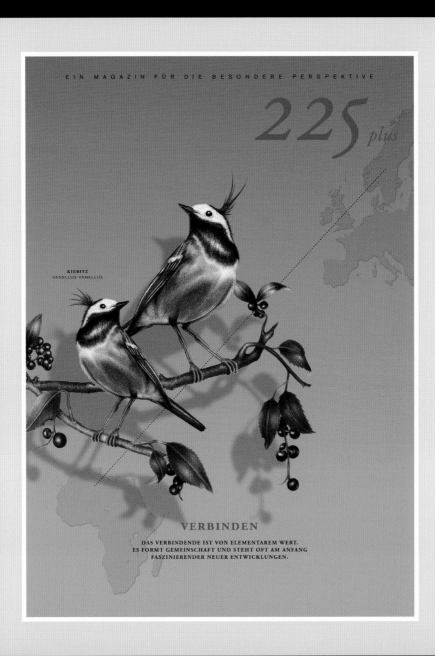

EIN MAGAZIN FÜR DIE BESONDERE PERSPEKTIVE

225 plus

KIEBITZ
VANELLUS VANELLUS

VERBINDEN

DAS VERBINDENDE IST VON ELEMENTAREM WERT.
ES FORMT GEMEINSCHAFT UND STEHT OFT AM ANFANG
FASZINIERENDER NEUER ENTWICKLUNGEN.

M A

G

ARNAUD
MAGGS:
PORTRAIT OF
A WORKING
ARTIST

onal

ARNAUD MAGGS

Arnaud Maggs (1926–2012) was an exceptional artist who had a humbling sense of awe for singular moments and the connections between them. Like other great photographers before him, he leaves behind a wealth of artistic creation that both challenges and enriches our understanding of the photographic medium. We worked closely with him on the design of the catalogue for *Identification*, a survey exhibition presented at the National Gallery of Canada.

G

Galle

X S

National Gallery of Canada /
Arnaud Maggs

L

J A

Pr

Edw

LE
JARDIN

LE
JARDIN

Le Jardin
Prince Edward
County

R

County

I N

Capturing the essence of a region and a chef's unique cuisine requires many talented people. For the branding of a proposed private restaurant in Prince Edward County, Ontario, we collaborated with photographers Jesse Senko and Michael Graydon, stylist Nikole Herriott, illustrator Melinda Josie and writer Doug Dolan.

S MAGAZINE

Joséphine
de La Baume
Edward Leida
Sagmeister & Walsh
Asger & Troels Carlsen   Hunters
Sebastian Black Iben Akerlie_ Jørgen Leth
IT /NL /BE /ES /PT /GR /CONT €17   AT €18.50

US$26.00
15>
2907407705
US $26.00

Acne

Gloves

Leggings: **PEACHOO + KREJBERG**

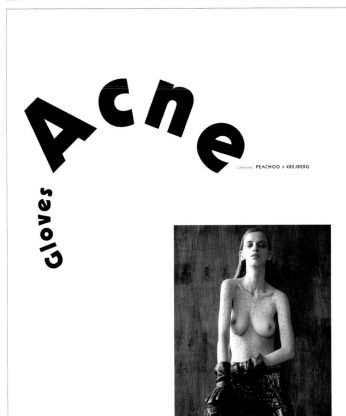

Dress: **HEXA BY KUHO**
Shoes: **AMAYA ARZUAGA**

Photographer **ROMAN GOEBEL** Stylist **DENNIS BLYS** Hair and Make-up **GREGOR MAKRIS**
Make **ALINA MIKHEEVA** Photo Assistant **JULIEN BARBES**

Theatre of Cruelty

Roman Goebel

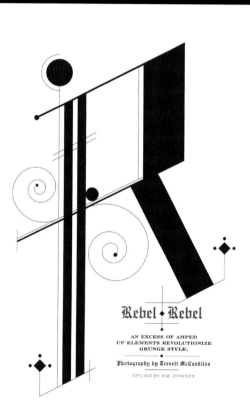

Rebel ◆ Rebel

AN EXCESS OF AMPED
UP ELEMENTS REVOLUTIONIZE
GRUNGE STYLE.

◆

Photography by Trevett McCandliss

STYLING BY KIM JOHNSON

Multi-strap Mary Jane
by **Modern Vice**, vintage
Betsey Johnson dress,
Southpaw plaid shirt, United,
Leggvee fishnet tights,
necklace by Rebel & Quill.

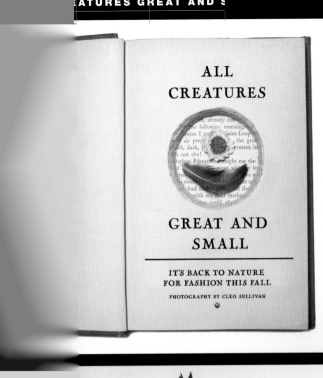

ALL CREATURES

GREAT AND SMALL

IT'S BACK TO NATURE
FOR FASHION THIS FALL

PHOTOGRAPHY BY CLEO SULLIVAN

STYLING BY MICHEL ONOFRIO

Le Tuit de la Lune cardigan, Lucky Fish T-shirt.

47

Carlo & Kind faux fur vest, La Miniatura dress, Emile et Ida tights, Minnetonka shoes; Zalkamoya jacket, Zutano zebra T-shirt, striped Oeuf arm warmers, Andy & Evan pants, Band of Bunnies shoes.

Opposite page, left to right: Antik Batik faux fur vest, Zalkamoya sweater, Oeuf knit pants, Minnetonka shoes; Oeuf sweater, Little Paul & Joe shorts, Emile et Ida tights, Band of Bunnies socks, Minnetonka shoes; sweater and blouse by Amelia, pants by Lucky Jade, vintage Fair Isle booties.

Style director: Michel Onofrio Hair and Makeup: Yuko Mizuno at Rona Rapmsents

57

The White Room Inc | Art Gallery of Mississauga

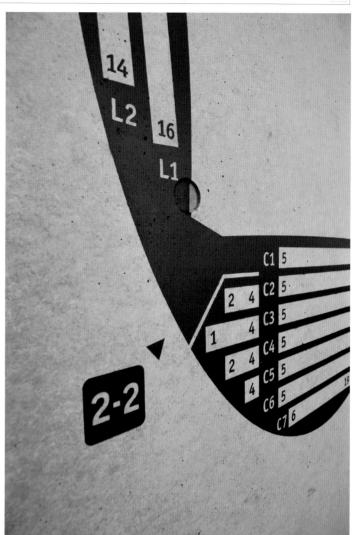

Lorenc+Yoo Design Inc | Hyatt Regency, New Orleans, LA.

Lorenc+Yoo Design Inc | Hyatt Regency, New Orleans, LA.

KMD Inc. | Council for Hakka Affairs

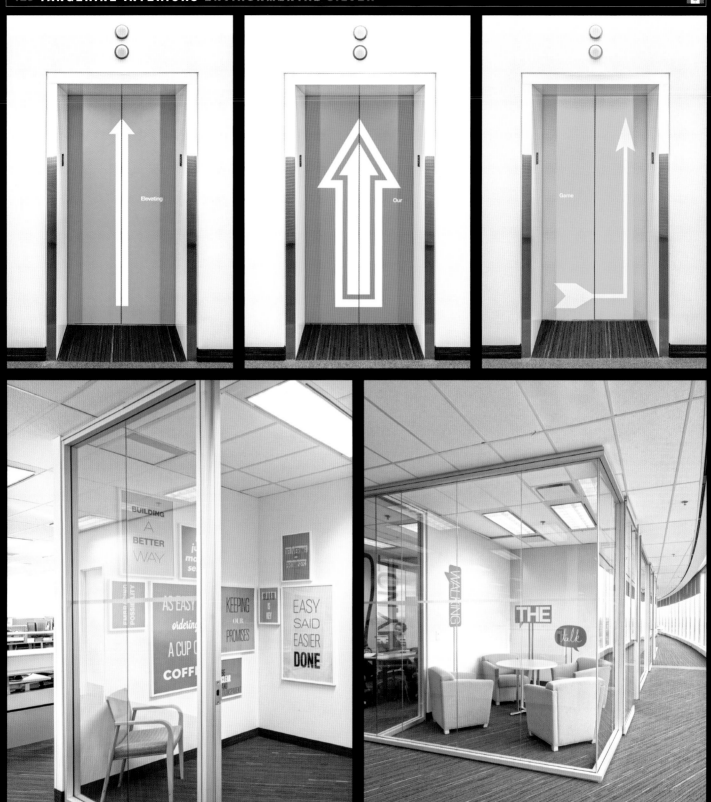

Regina Rubino / Robert Louey | Rosewood London

Regina Rubino / Robert Louey | Rosewood London

Poulin + Morris Inc. | **Granum A/I**

Set in Neue Haas Grotesk
Display Std 75 Bold

TOMERS TRUST RESPECT DIGNITY INTEGRITY PEOPL

a cleaner tomorrow

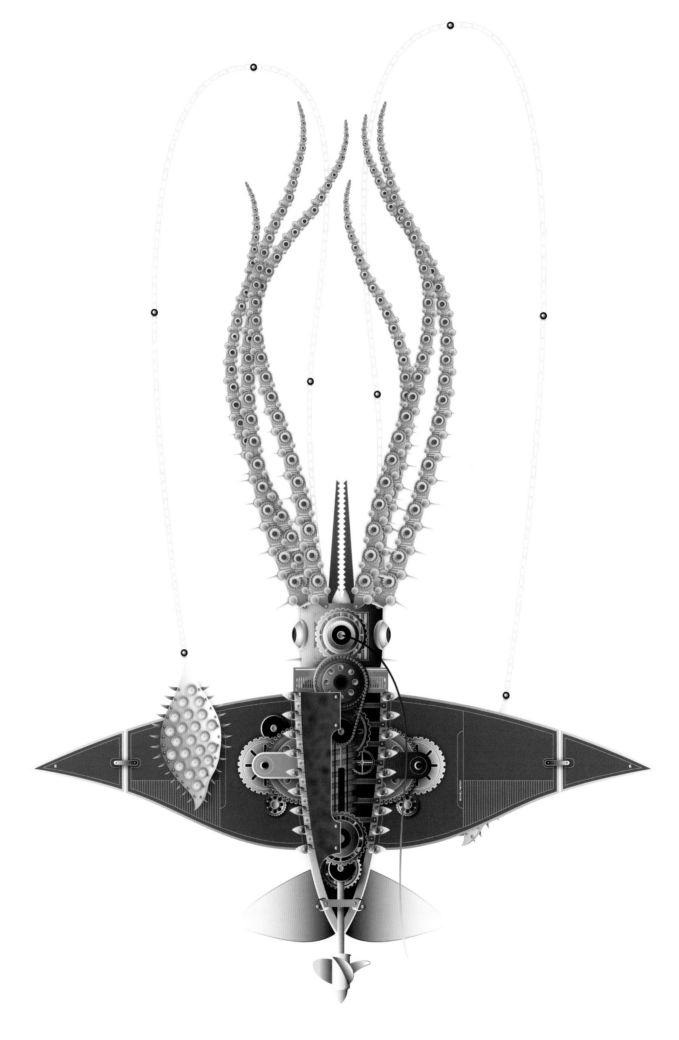

I will be gone soon. Under what circumstances, I cannot declare with precision. I am running out of time. My last few nights have been restless... sometimes I feel as if I have already turned...

As my personal fate faces much uncertainty, it is perhaps worth noting: while all my devices have developed in conjunction with the VELOSTER TURBO, I have diligently customized them for proper fitting on a larger vehicle, as well as one with a smaller framework. May those who survive me duly apply them for their own use, non-partisan to vessel type.

If this is my end, I can say with all my heart that I tried... As for my successors, now there is hope... I just pray they find it.....

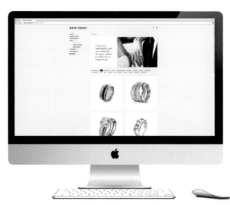

The White Room Inc | Erin Tracy

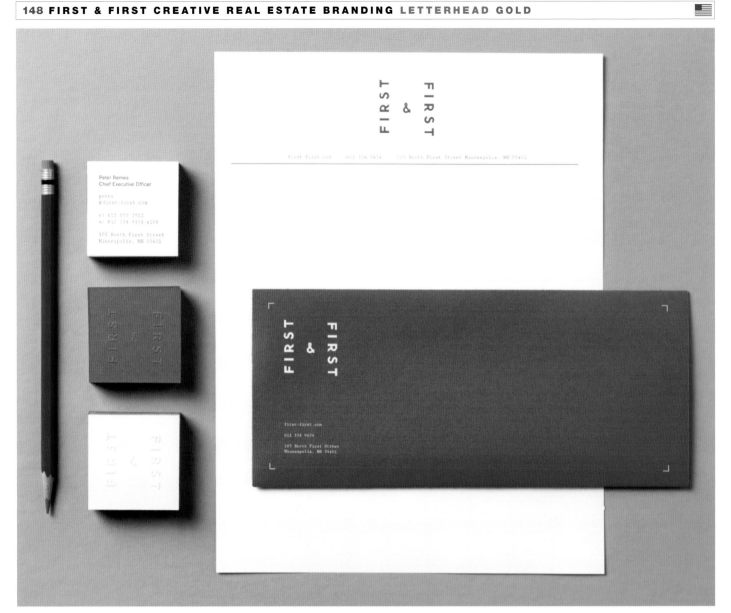

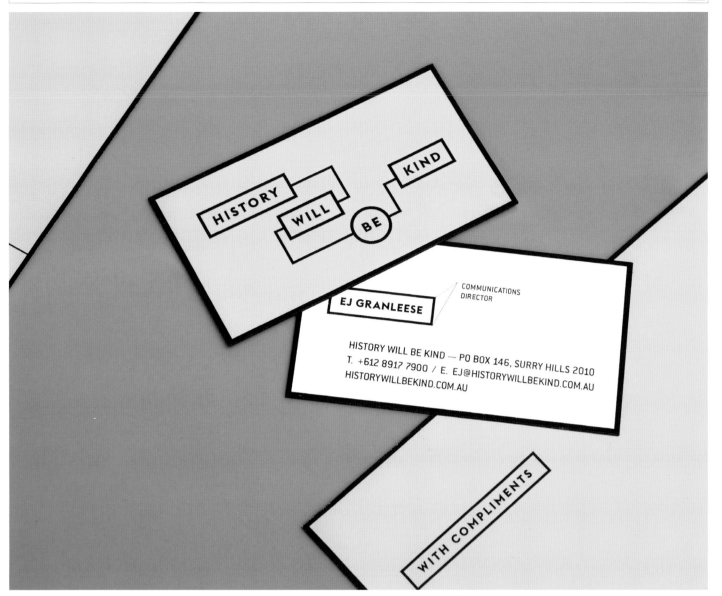

Peppermill Projects | Old Ox Brewery

Michael Schwab Studio | Angels & Cowboys, Yoav Gilat

   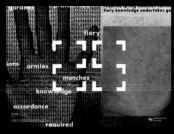

 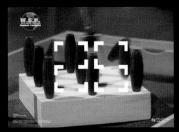  

The Partners | Film and Video Umbrella

Graham Hanson Design | Google New York

Odear | Odear Open

Liquid Agency | Ficks

Mermaid, Inc. | digital arts

The General Design Co. | Tenth and Page Realty

Alt Group | New Zealand Opera

Design is Play | Los Angeles Boulders

Bailey Lauerman | Nebraska Antique Farming Association

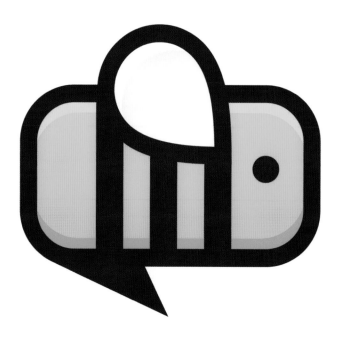

Squires & Company | Yumblebee

Craig-Teerlink Design | MapR Technologies

Design is Play | Touchstone Climbing

Hawkeye Communications | Sundance Construction

AG Creative | Palmieri Bros Paving

Leynivopnid | Sisters

Toolbox Design | Anthony Gismondi

Flake | Event Academy

H.Tuncay Design | "A Trip to the Moon" Film and Production Company

Michael Schwab Studio | Peet's Coffee & Tea

The General Design Co. | Caffe Aficionado

H.Tuncay Design | "Red Bracer" production company

Chase Design Group | **Rose Cole**

Leap | **Kestrel Aircraft**

Pentagram | **Waller Creek Revitalization Initiative**

mkcreative | **Turett Architect**

xose teiga, studio. | **Clinic Blanco Ramos**

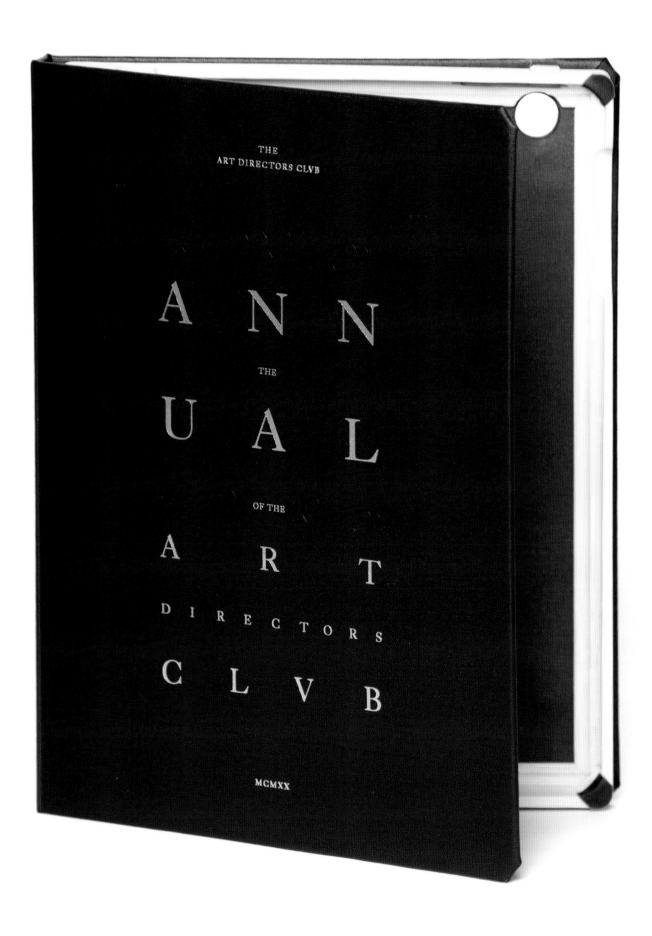

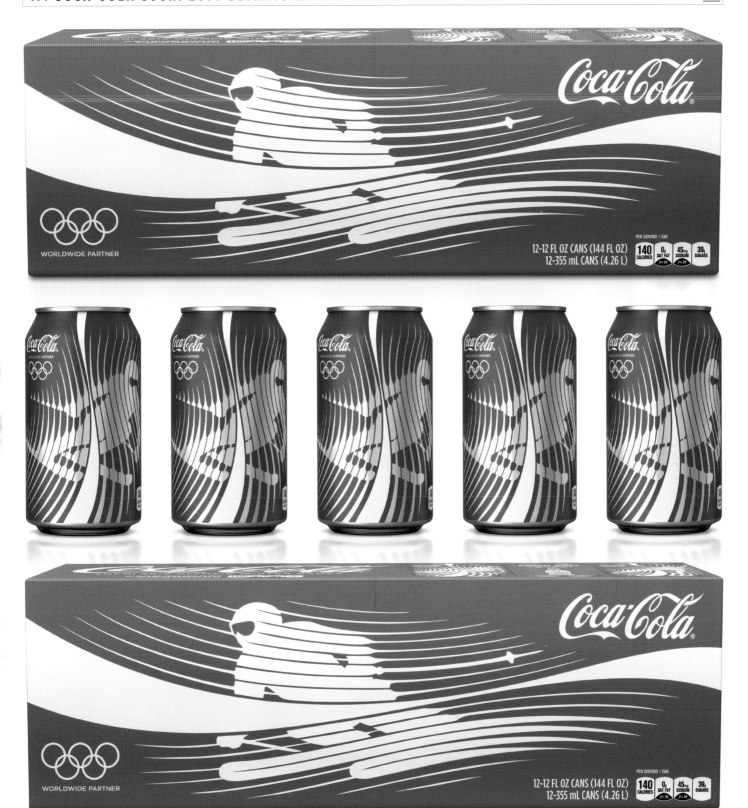

Turner Duckworth Design: London & San Francisco | The Coca-Cola Company North America

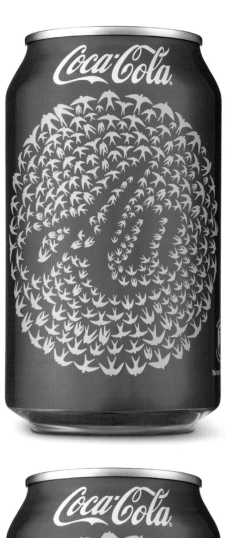

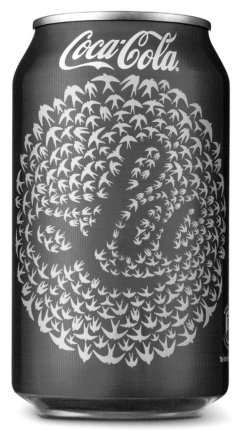
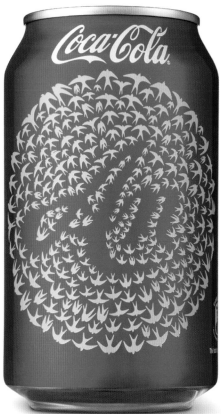

Rice Creative | Coca-Cola

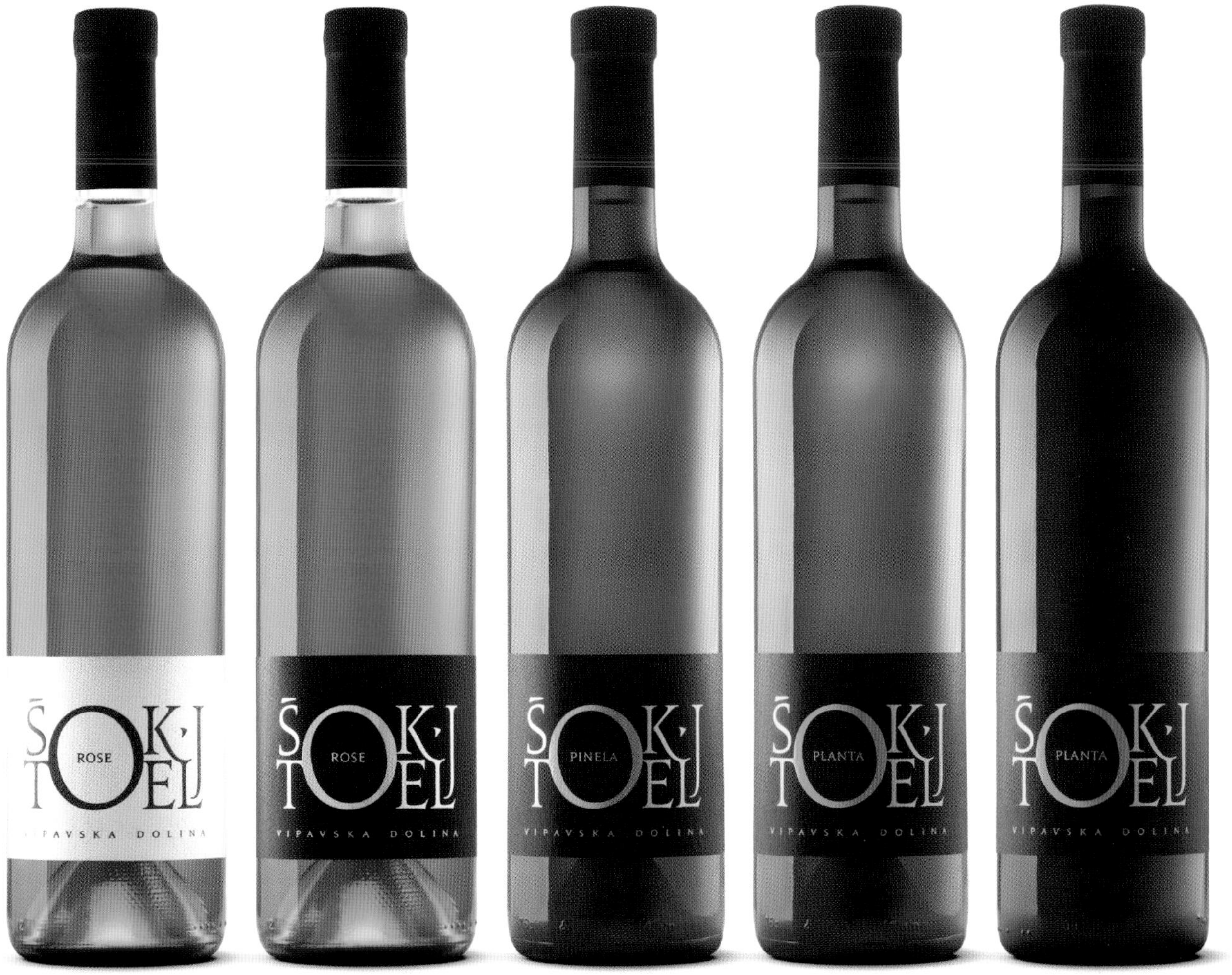

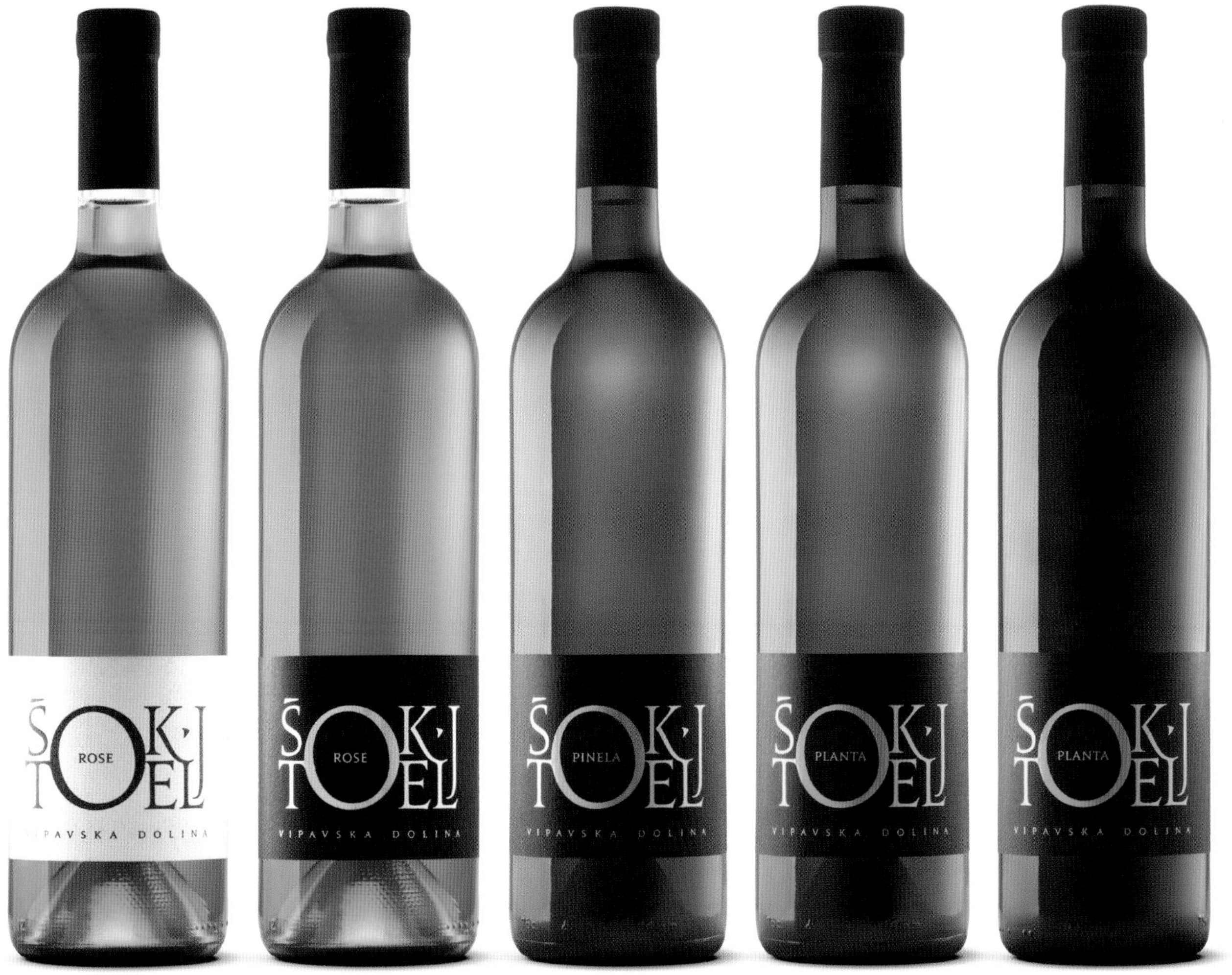

Spela Draslar S.P. | Stokelj wines

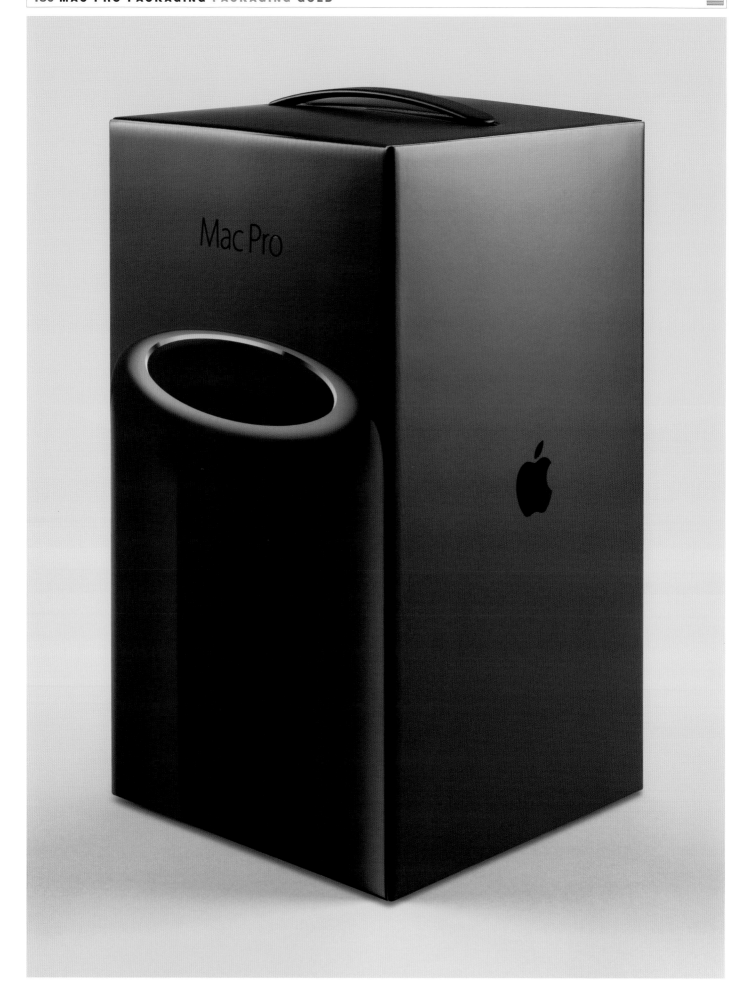

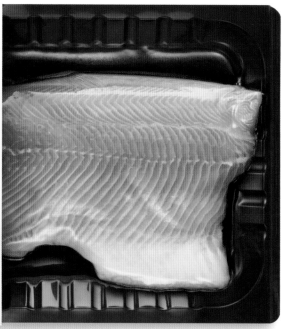

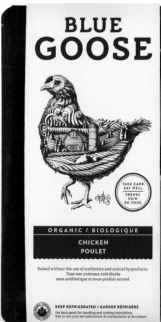

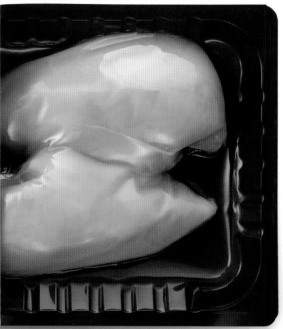

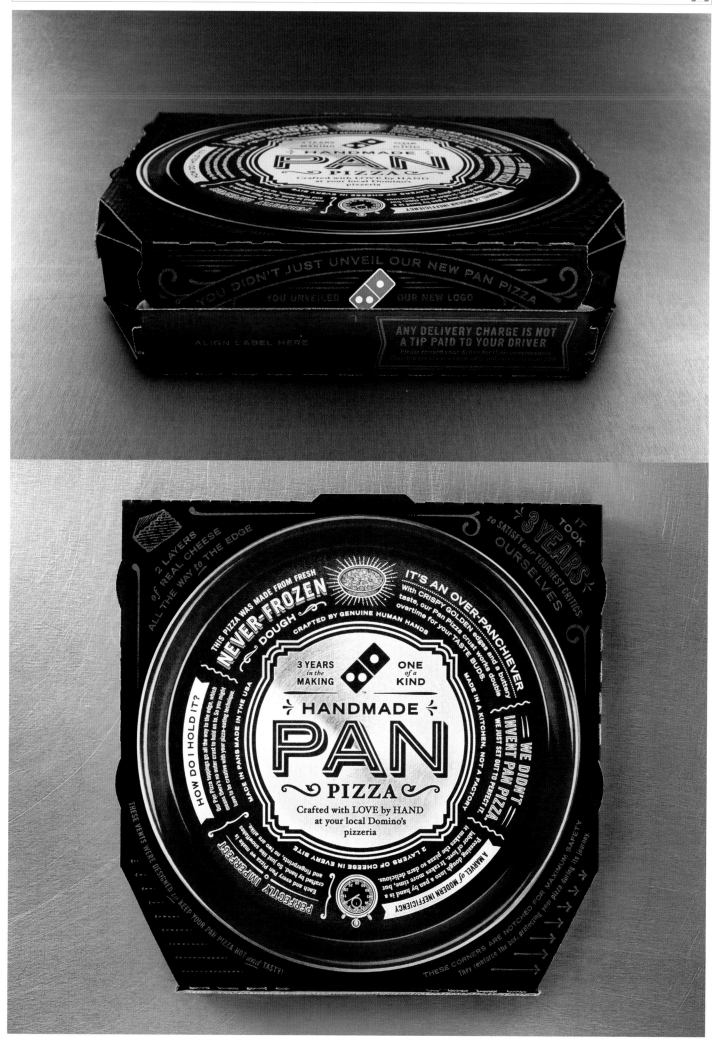

Sagmeister & Walsh, Visual Arts Press, Ltd. | School of Visual Arts

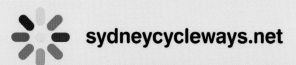

sydneycycleways.net

sydneycycleways.net

CITY OF SYDNEY 2030

Frost* Design | City Of Sydney

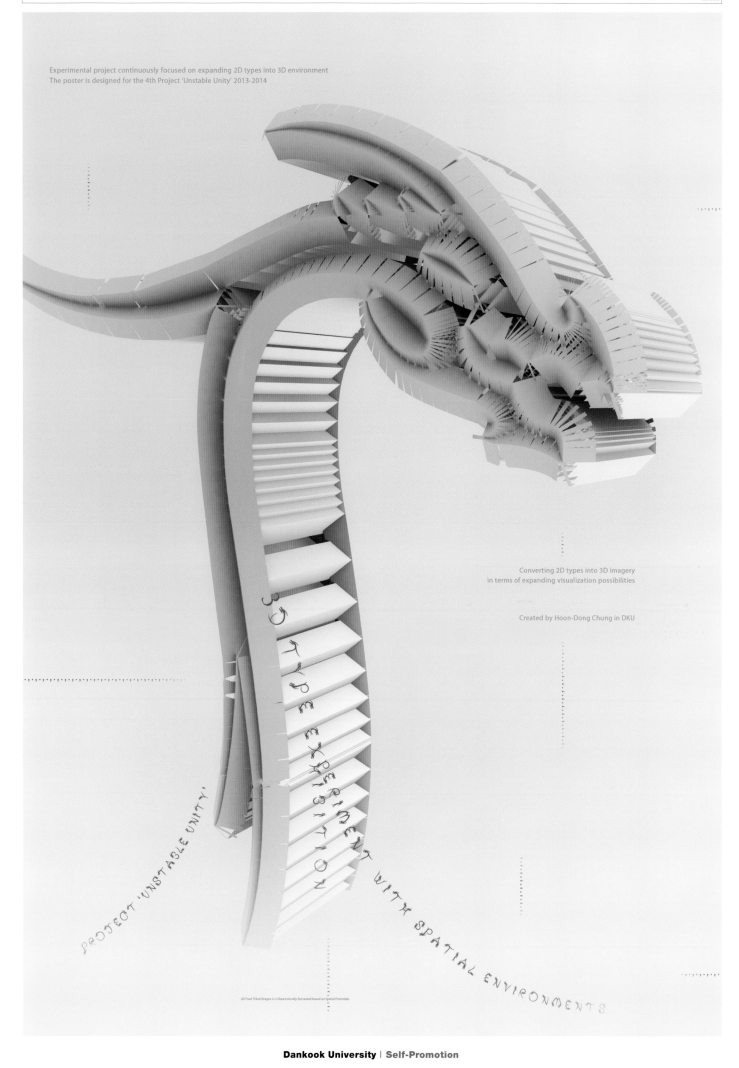

Experimental project continuously focused on expanding 2D types into 3D environment
The poster is designed for the 4th Project 'Unstable Unity' 2013-2014

Converting 2D types into 3D imagery
in terms of expanding visualization possibilities

Created by Hoon-Dong Chung in DKU

peter bankov | **Teatr-Teatr. Theatrical center from Perm.**

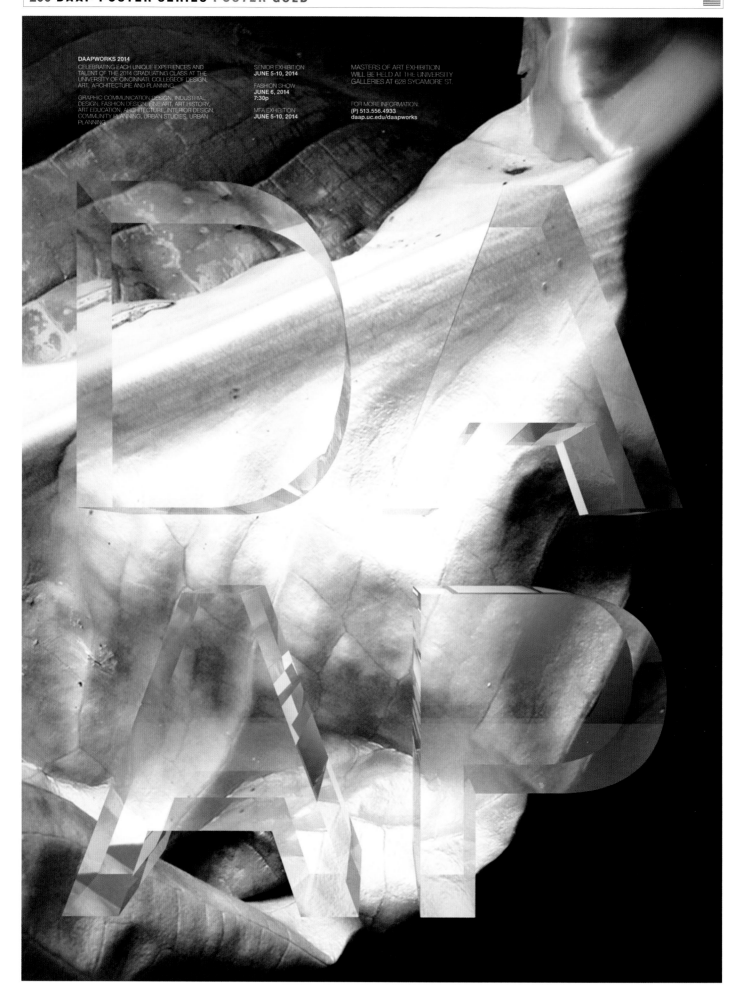

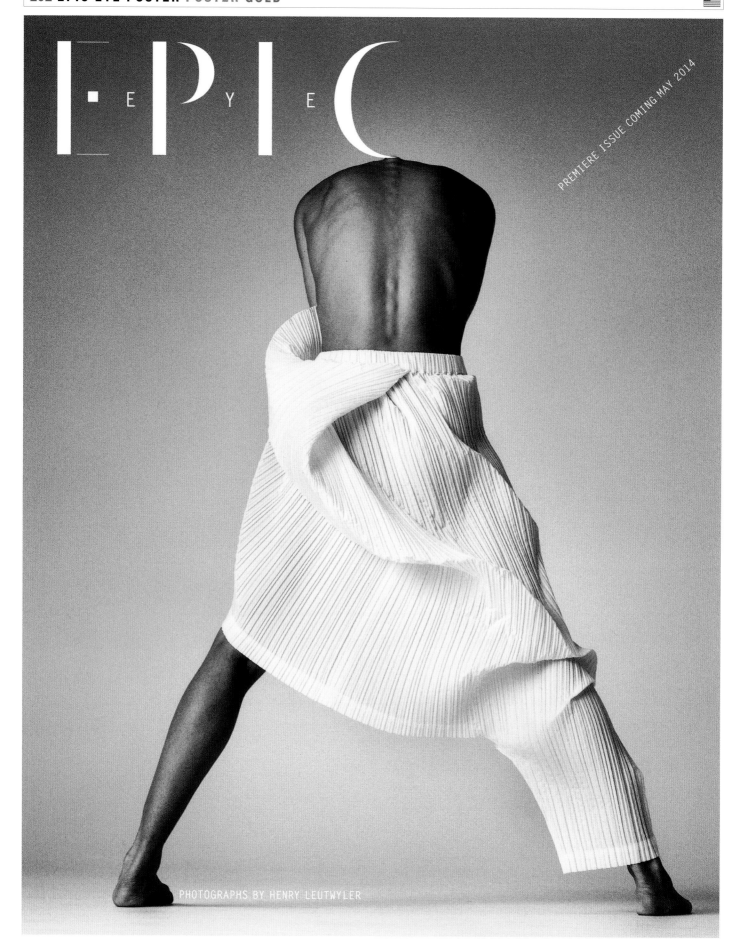

PREMIERE ISSUE COMING MAY 2014

PHOTOGRAPHS BY HENRY LEUTWYLER

MAXIMUM DIVIDE

ON MINIMUM WAGE

STATE LEGISLATURES
Read about it in this month's issue

STATE LEGISLATURES
Read about it in this month's issue

601 Design, Inc. | National Conference of State Legislatures

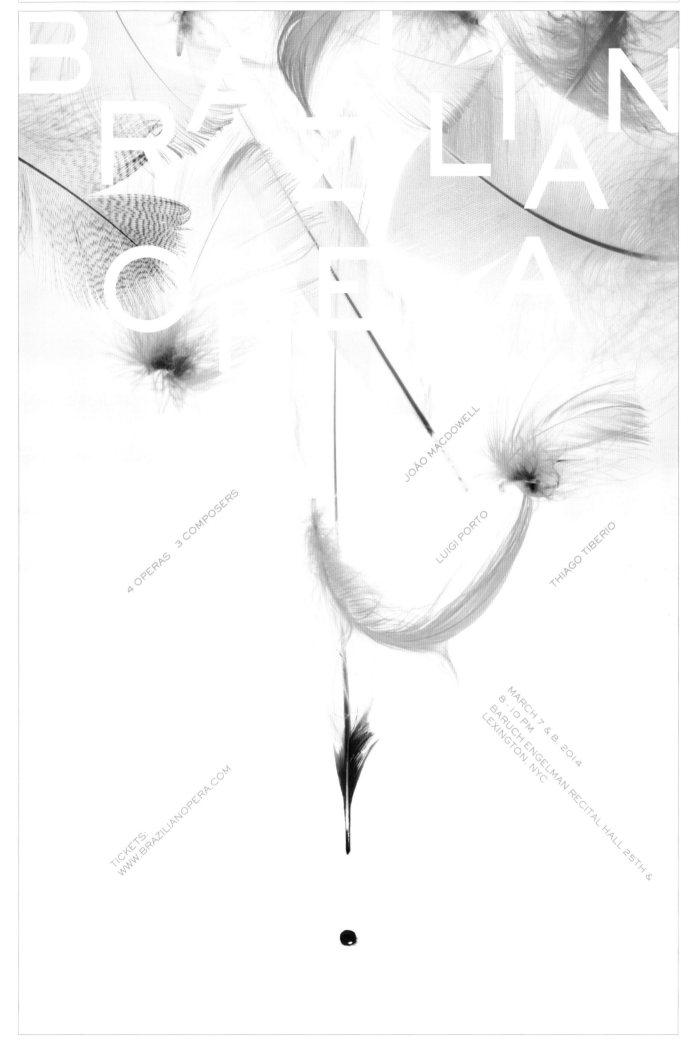

Brazilian Opera

4 OPERAS 3 COMPOSERS

JOÃO MACDOWELL

LUIGI PORTO

THIAGO TIBERIO

TICKETS:
WWW.BRAZILIANOPERA.COM

MARCH 7 & 8. 2014
8 - 10 PM
BARUCH ENGELMAN RECITAL HALL 25TH &
LEXINGTON. NYC

IF Studio | International Brazilian Opera Company

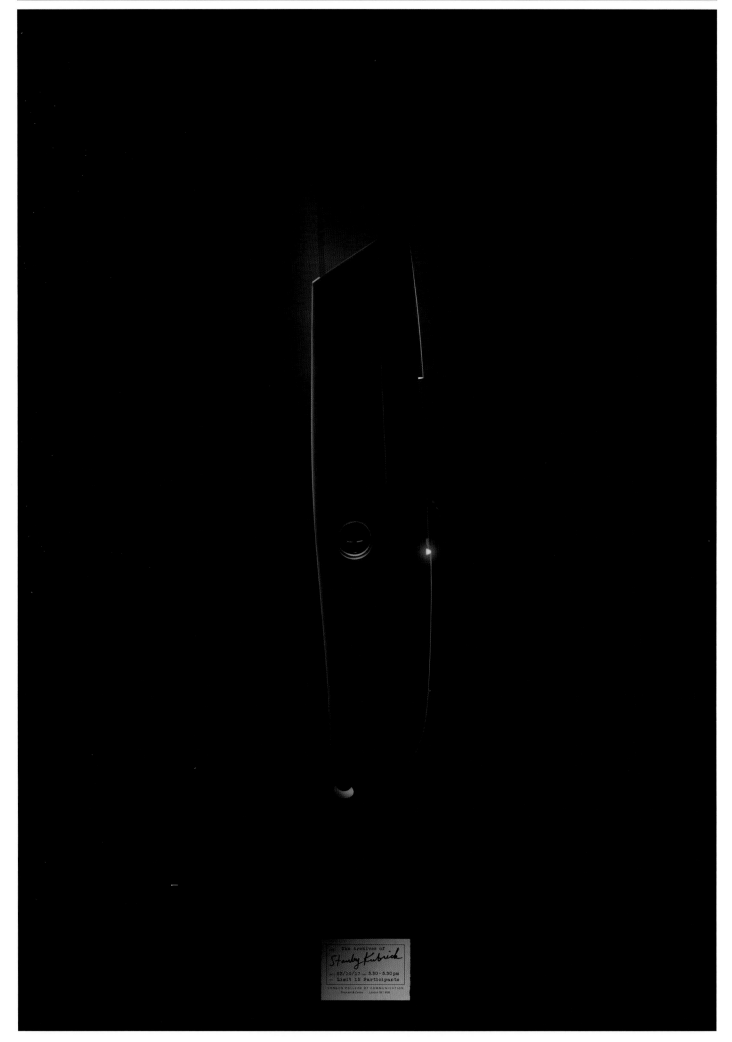

Landor Associates | Stanley Kubrick Archive

omdr Co.,Ltd. | MTG Co.,Ltd.

SPRING SERIES 2014
THE UNIVERSITY OF TEXAS AT AUSTIN
SCHOOL OF ARCHITECTURE

SYMPOSIA

TEX-FAB 5, SKIN: DIGITAL ASSEMBLIES
FEBRUARY 19-23
tex-fab.net/

NATURE AND CITIES:
URBAN ECOLOGICAL DESIGN AND PLANNING
FEBRUARY 28-MARCH 1
soa.utexas.edu/calendar/natureandcities

LATITU6ES:
A SYMPOSIUM ON ARCHITECTURE IN THE AMERICAS
APRIL 3-4

EXHIBITIONS

CARET6
FEBRUARY 1-18
RECEPTION FEBRUARY 7

3xLP
FEBRUARY 18-28
TEX-FAB EXHIBITION RECEPTION FEBRUARY 21

All exhibitions are held in Goldsmith Mebane Gallery, open Monday to Friday,
8:00am to 5:00pm.

All lectures are at 5:00pm in Goldsmith Hall 3.120 unless otherwise noted.
Goldsmith Hall is located at 22nd & Guadalupe.

Events are subject to change. For updates, visit soa.utexas.edu.

Design by Dyal and Partners

SPEAKERS

JEROLD KAYDEN
HARVARD UNIVERSITY
GRADUATE SCHOOL OF DESIGN
JANUARY 22

TOD WILLIAMS AND BILLIE TSIEN
TOD WILLIAMS BILLIE TSIEN ARCHITECTS
JANUARY 29
JESSEN AUDITORIUM

JULIE EIZENBERG
KONINGEIZENBERG ARCHITECTURE
FEBRUARY 5

GEORGE CHARLES GALSTER
WAYNE STATE UNIVERSITY
FEBRUARY 12

GINA REICHERT AND MITCH COPE
DESIGN 99
FEBRUARY 17

MICHEL ROJKIND
ROJKIND ARQUITECTOS
FEBRUARY 20
JESSEN AUDITORIUM

STEFAN BEHNISCH
BEHNISCH ARCHITEKTEN
MARCH 17

DAVID ELALOUF
ADE ARCHITECTES/ATELIER DAVID ELALOUF
APRIL 9

ROLAND SNOOKS
STUDIO ROLAND SNOOKS
APRIL 21

THE ARTISTS HAVE CHECKED IN.

Illustration Art Exhibition | March 6th–30th | Gladstonehotel.com/spaces/iwct

GLADSTONE
HOTEL

Sydney Rogers, LLC. | Sydney Rogers

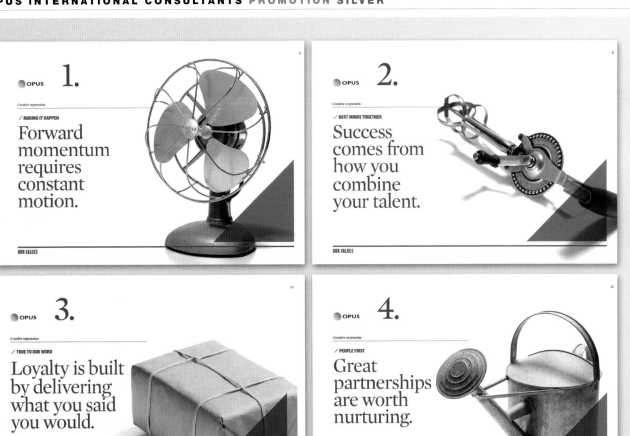

Laurie Frankel Photography | *Self-Promotion*

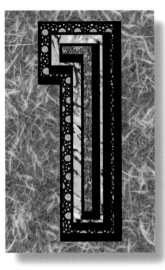

AlphaChrome
A DESIGNER SET OF 39 POSTCARDS
FEATURING LETTERS, NUMBERS & SYMBOLS
IN DECORATIVE PATTERNS.

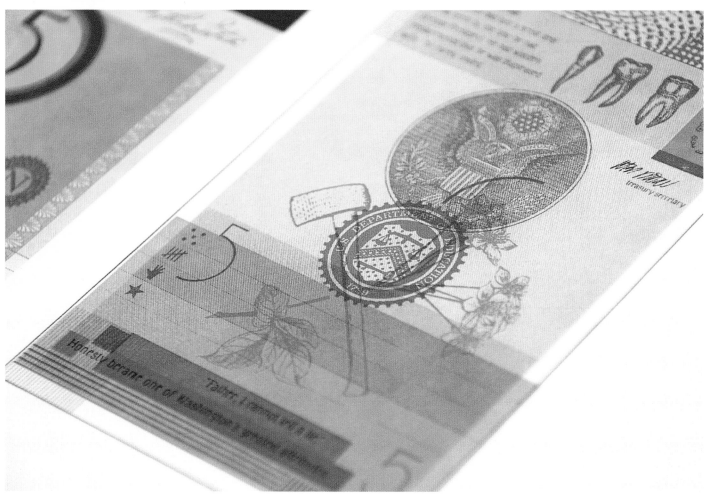

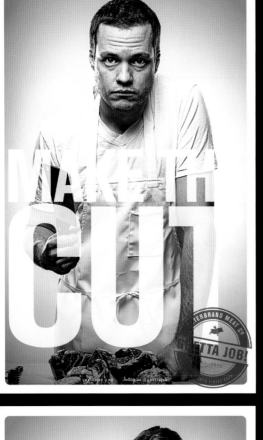

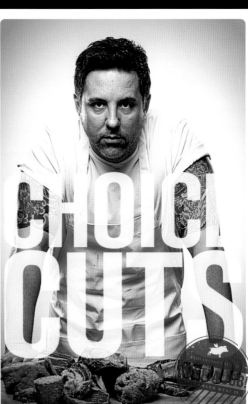

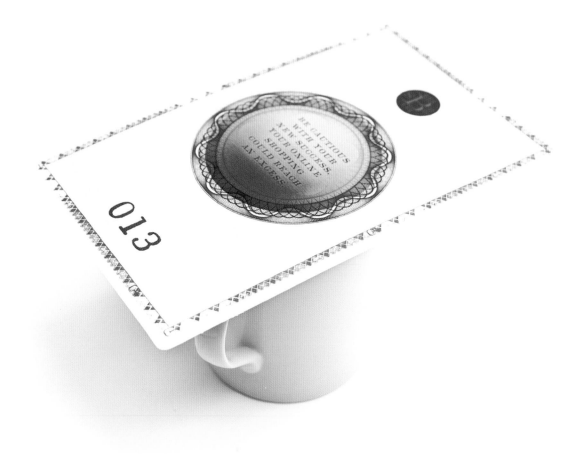

An insult to squash this sugary seasonal brew
Fans more obscene than any of Bacchus' krewe
Be happy with pie and bread
Avoid the stomachache instead

STIR DRINK IN THE SUNSET'S WAY
TO QUIET THE CRAZE OF PUMPKIN SPICE LATTE

*Abuse of social media symbols
turns updaters into oversharing fou
One use per instance
Is enough to feign importance*

WAVE MUG OVER SMARTPHONE
AND TOO MUCH HASHTAGGING SHALL BE UNKOWN

SHAMELESS IS T
FROM KINDA SO
PASSÉ ARE TH
RESTORED ARE

CIRCLE M
AND T

003 NO

LE SOLITAIRE FORK
—JUICE CLEANSES—

006

ESSENCE OF KALE, PARSLEY AND BEET
MAKE A DESOLE SUBSTITUTE FOR MEAT
BRAGGERS OF A LIQUIDS-ONLY DIET
FOOD SHALL FINALLY MAKE QUIET

BLOW TWICE THE STEAM FROM CUP
AND JUICE CLEANSERS WILL
KINDLY EAT UP

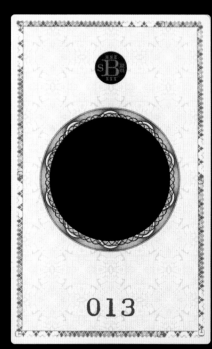

013

LA EN
—H

*A beauty pa
Needn't such a su
Shut the pry
Their own lif*

TAP FILL
HONEY BOO

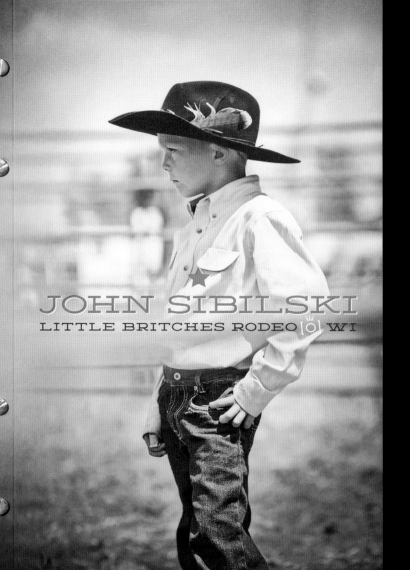

JOHN SIBILSKI
LITTLE BRITCHES RODEO [O] WI

414.405.4607 · JOHN@JOHNSIBILSKI.COM

PROPOSITION
CHICKEN

1 CHOOSE YOUR CHICKEN

A **FRIED**
mary's free-range fried chicken,
buttermilk marinade

B **FLIPPED**
mary's free-range slow-roasted
rotisserie chicken, lemon, garlic,
italian parsley marinade

C **FAKE**
crispy bbq tofu

2 CHOOSE YOUR STYLE

A **SANDWICH**
amoroso hearth-baked roll, mayo, $10
spicy slaw, thyme & sage potato chips

B **SALAD**
kale, cucumber, cherry tomatoes, $11
mint, carrots, agrumato vinaigrette

C **ENTREE**
buttermilk biscuit, honey butter, $12
spicy slaw

PROVISIONS

ANISETTE #1

Webster | Jones Bros. Cupcakes

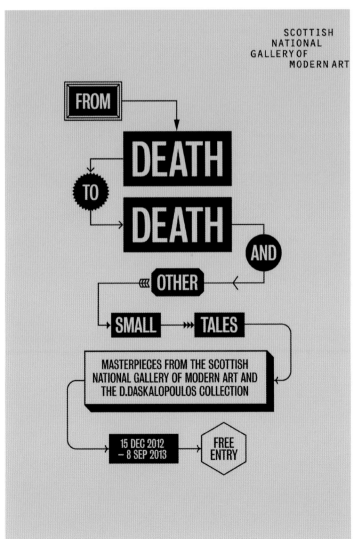

JANUARY FEBRUARY MARCH APRIL MAY JUNE JULY AUGUST SEPTEMBER OCTOBER NOVEMBER DECEMBER

01 JAN	NEW YEAR'S DAY
13 JAN	COMING OF AGE DAY
11 FEB	NATIONAL FOUNDATION DAY
21 MAR	SPRING EQUINOX
29 APR	SHOWA DAY
03 MAY	CONSTITUTION MEMORIAL DAY
04 MAY	GREENERY DAY
05 MAY	CHILDREN'S DAY
06 MAY	"GREENERY DAY" OBSERVED
21 JUL	MARINE DAY
15 SEP	RESPECT FOR THE AGED DAY
23 SEP	AUTUMN EQUINOX
13 OCT	SPORTS DAY
03 NOV	CULTURE DAY
23 NOV	LABOR THANKSGIVING DAY
24 NOV	"LABOR THANKSGIVING DAY" OBSERVED
23 DEC	EMPEROR'S BIRTHDAY

2014 CALENDAR

JAPANESE EDITION
—
COPYRIGHT © 2012-2014
KRIMTH INC. ALL RIGHTS RESERVED

NAIL ART PRODUCTS

KEI TAKIMOTO | Krimth Inc.

Credits & Commentary

20, 21 INTELLECTA ANNUAL REPORT 2012 | Design Firm: Intellecta Corporate
Client: Intellecta | Designer: Anders Schmidt | Photographers: Tim Flach, Magnus Mårding
Assignment: The Company is undergoing major changes in shift of business focus, sale of an entire Business Area and a new CEO. The theme of the Annual Report is "Metamorphos," which is boldly stated in matt varnish from back to front on the cover's glossy image. The "morp" part of the word is also the abbreviation of the Company's Values.
Approach: The Annual Report has six different covers using six different pupea, the stage between two life forms. The theme of ongoing change from print to digital is coherent in text as well as images. For example, the spread with the morphed images of the retiring to the newly appointed CEO. The mix of uncoated and glossy paper, the smaller size of the image sheets and the generous format gives the report a classic, yet exclusive and modern feel.
Results: Very well received both internally and externally. Following the Company's shift from print to digital, this is most likely Intellecta's last printed annual report. This is going out in style.

22 ISTAR FINANCIAL ANNUAL REPORT 2012 | Design Firm: Addison
Client: iStar Financial | Designer: Chelsea Podlogar | Creative Director: Richard Colbourne

23 CENVEO 2012 ANNUAL REPORT | Design Firm: Addison | Client: Cenveo
Designer: Kin Yuen | Creative Director: Richard Colbourne

24, 25 THE UNIVERSITY OF HARTFORD, HARTFORD ART SCHOOL RECRUITMENT PACKAGE | Design Firm: 160over90 | Client: The University of Hartford, Hartford Art School
Designers: Kay Sim, Chad Miller | Production Manager: Mary Olson
Printer: J.S. McCarthy Printers | Photographers: Tom Ammon, Ryan Greenberg
Executive Creative Director: Jim Walls | Creative Director: Sig Gross
Copywriter: Chara Odhner | Chief Creative Officer: Darryl Cilli
Associate Creative Director: Travis Ludwig

26 UNICEF ZEROAWARD | Design Firm: Rice Creative | Client: UNICEF
Designer: Kornelia Engqvist | Creative Directors: Chi-An De Leo and Joshua Breidenbach

27 TROPHY - CÂNDIDO DE OLIVEIRA SUPER CUP | Design Firm: Nuno Duarte Martins
Client: Portuguese Football Federation | Designer: Nuno Duarte Martins
Production: Vista Alegre Atlantis, Domingos Guedes Lda | Photographer: Diogo Pinto (FPF)
Assignment: The Portuguese Football Federation commissioned Nuno Duarte Martins to oversee the design of a new trophy for the season opening of the Cândido de Oliveira Super Cup match. The match was played between the winners of the Portuguese national championship and the Portuguese Cup. With a view to boost the prestige of the match, we were briefed to create a trophy that is striking, singular and symbolic.
Approach: The first job was to understand the reasons that led the Portuguese Football Federation to commission a new cup, and put ideas on paper. The process of drawing up the first sketches, gaining approval and converting the plans into the 3D version of the trophy involved two months of hard work. The trophy represents a game between champions, a grand final between the national champions and the winner of the Portuguese Cup. It comprises two silver parts connected by a crystal piece, the only symmetrical part of the trophy, symbolizing the spirit of Cândido de Oliveira (after whom the match is named) and fair play. The etching on the top of the crystal depicts the spectacular nature of the game and the fight to triumph in the match, through players' movements and golden lines that embrace the five Portuguese quinas – the heraldic shields on the Portuguese flag. The larger silver piece on the right represents the winners, the one of the left the defeated team. The position of these two pieces in the trophy as a whole and the respective cuts form the Cross of Christ, representing the last crusade, the final conquest. The intention was to make an analogy to the Portuguese conquests, alluding to a golden period in Portugal's history. All the past winners of the Super Cup are listed on the back of the trophy, on the silver piece dedicated to the winners, and each year the name of the respective winner will be added. The highly intricate design of the trophy required meticulous teamwork. The main challenge was to produce the large crystal component. The prestigious Portuguese company Vista Alegre Atlantis (founded in 1824) produced the crystal piece. In its long history the company had never before created such a large crystal. The complex process was carried out manually almost in its entirety and required 100 kilos of raw crystal! It was a high-risk project, above all because of the painstaking production of the crystal. A battery of tests was carried out on a multitude of pieces (many were broken) and on several occasions it was thought the trophy was unfeasible!
Results: The launch of the trophy had a big impact on public opinion and earned widespread praise in the national and international press. As well as its stunning appearance, the trophy also proved to be functional. Given that crystal is a heavy material several solutions were tested to make sure the trophy was not too weighty and could be handled easily.
Proof of the design's success came on the day it was unveiled during the winning team's celebrations. The spectacular and photogenic nature of the trophy as well as its functionality became apparent for all to see.

28, 29 S. | Design Firm: Headcase Design | Client: Melcher Media /Mulholland Books /Bad Robot | Designers: Paul Kepple, Ralph Geroni | Website: www.headcasedesign.com
Production Manager: Kurt Andrews | Hand Lettering: Lynne Ciccaglione, Megan Worman
Editor: Lauren Nathan | Authors: Doug Dorst, J.J. Abrams | Art Director: Paul Kepple
Assignment: "S." is the first novel conceived by film maker J. J. Abrams and written by Doug Dorst, envisioned as a literary mystery box: One book. Two readers. A world of mystery, menace, and desire. A young woman picks up a book left behind by a stranger. Inside it are his margin notes, which reveal a reader entranced by the story and by its mysterious author. She responds with notes of her own, leaving the book for the stranger, and so begins an unlikely conversation that plunges them both into the unknown. The book: "Ship of Theseus," published in 1949, the final novel by a prolific but enigmatic writer named V.M. Straka, in which a man with no past is shanghaied onto a strange ship with a monstrous crew and launched onto a disorienting and perilous journey.
Approach: To intrigue the reader and imply its mysterious and interactive nature, the book comes sealed with a sticker in a black on black foil stamped slipcase. After breaking the seal, the book that is revealed is "Ship Of Theseus," the stolen library book. Upon opening, you discover that the book has been heavily annotated — the handwriting in the margins tells the story of the two college students. The stolen book is used as a communication device between the students as they pass it back and forth. Tucked inside the pages of the book are 20 plus pieces of removable ephemera (custom designed for this book) which provide clues and sub-stories, including a map drawn on an actual napkin, postcards, photos, letters, a funeral card, a college newspaper, mimeographed telegrams, Xeroxed documents, and even a decoder wheel. J. J. Abrams was adamant about keeping the experience as realistic as possible for the reader so they become immersed in the Meta world of the novel. Each piece of ephemera was printed on the most realistic paper stock possible (newsprint for the campus newspaper, bible paper, and an actual paper napkin). Every detail needed to be addressed — fake isbn number and company logo on the back of the greeting card, realistic Brazilian postage for the postcards, creating an identity system for the imaginary Pollard State University. An actual sticker was used for the library sticker on the spine. A custom "S" was created as a symbol for the secret society depicted in the story (used prominently on the slipcase). Time-specific fonts were researched and chosen to set the books text (New Caledonia), and all writing in the margins is authentic handwriting.
Results: The book was well received with both critics and audiences, becoming a "New York Times" bestseller and finding an audience willing to embrace and participate in it's challenges. There are different ways to approach reading the book, and it is up to the reader how they wish to tackle it. There have been numerous websites and blogs by fans dedicated to decoding the mysteries of the novel. Many people comment that the book can be enjoyed as an intriguing object even if you don't spend the time reading and deciphering the book. It was very rewarding to work on a book that celebrates the medium of print—a book whose experience can't be duplicated in a digital realm.

30, 31 108 ROCK STAR GUITARS | Design Firm: SMOG Design, Inc.
Client: Lisa S. Johnson | Designer: Nick Steinhardt | Editor: Eric Laster
Creative Director: Jeri Heiden | Art Director: Nick Steinhardt
Websites: www.108rockstarguitars.com, www.smogdesign.com

32, 33 CITY ABANDONED, CHARTING THE LOSS OF CIVIC INSTITUTIONS IN PHILADELPHIA | Design Firm: 21xdesign | Client: Paul Dry Books | Designer: Dermot Mac Cormack
Writers: Vincent Feldman, John Andrew Gallery, Kenneth Finkel
Production Manager: Will Schofield | Photographer: Vincent Feldman
Editor-in-Chief: Paul Dry | Editor: John Corenswet
Art Directors: Dermot Mac Cormack, Patricia McElroy

34, 35 ARQUITECTURA COM AUTOR (ARCHITECTURE WITH AUTHOR)
Design Firm: White Studio | Client: Câmara Municipal de Guimarães
– Arquivo Municipal Alfredo Pimenta | Designers: Ana Simões, Raquel Rei, Jorge Amador
Art Director: Eduardo Aires

36, 37 SURF TEXAS | Design Firm: Pentagram
Client: Kenny Braun/University of Texas Press | Designer: Barrett Fry | Art Director: DJ Stout

38, 39 RETOOLING AND REINVIGORATING AMERICA'S ORIGINAL DIY BRAND
Design Firm: Lippincott | Client: BLACK + DECKER | Designer: Marc Hohmann, Sam Ayling, Imri Larsen | Strategy/Naming: Amit Sabharwal, Benjamin Grant
Strategy Director: Steve Lawrence | Production: Jeremy Darty, Brendan deVallance
Photographer: David Arky | Creative Director: Marc Hohmann
Assignment: In 2013, Stanley Black & Decker engaged us to help redefine their brand. We outlined clear — and demanding — objectives for the brand strategy and design: the brand would need to be fundamentally human, to reflect BLACK + DECKER's ability to transform a daunting task into a feeling of accomplishment. It would need to be simple, while still being meaningfully different and modern. More tactically, the brand would need to be versatile enough to shape a cohesive end-to-end customer journey and explicit enough to bring unity to a broad product portfolio and visual system.
Approach: Together, these objectives defined a brand strategy that revolves around BLACK + DECKER's legacy and future of empowering consumers all over the world to transform their homes, their communities, and their lives. Over the course of months, we worked with the BLACK + DECKER team to understand the business' strategic trajectory, spending time with consumers around the globe. We studied design evolution to better understand the brand's resonance with trends like post-hastism and the market's rediscovered demand for pure craftsmanship. We iteratively defined a strategy and design that embraces the brand's heritage, signals the brand's future, and is a brand for today's world.
Results: The goal of the new positioning and visual identity was to represent the vast array of products that BLACK + DECKER offers. The logo aims to strike the perfect balance between all of the brands' categories: it maintains the signature masculine, orange black palette for power tools and outdoor products, but receives a softer and more elegant treatment for products used inside the home, using a white and grey color palette. The uppercase, stacked type is technical and sharp; the round edges of the holding shape are soft and flexible.

40 KIRKSTALL BREWERY BRANDING | Design Firm: WPA Pinfold | Client: Kirkstall Brewery
Designers: Myles Pinfold, Chris McMahon, Emma Rutherford, Hayley Wall
Assignment: Kirkstall Brewery was formed in 2010 by Steve Holt, a passionate advocate of craft beer. The opening of the brewery coincided with a period of deep economic recession, increasing beer tax and a record number of pub closures. In addition, there has been a boom in microbreweries and Kirkstall's core regional market (Yorkshire) has more microbreweries than any other region. The brief was to create a brand that has provenance and reinforces the craft and traditional brewing values of this regional brewery, as well as adding value and standing out in a very crowded and highly competitive market.
Approach: Creating a new craft brewery brand in this environment was challenging.

Credits & Commentary 238

Credits & Commentary

It had to stand out from the crowded market place in a credible way and build on the provenance of its name – inspired by Kirkstall Abbey and the brewing prowess of the Cistercian monks. In addition, the brand identity needed to add value at a time when the market has been flooded with microbreweries competing on price, and the price of a pint of beer has increased considerably. The brand design takes its inspiration from the style of manuscripts that would have been produced by the Cistercian monks who inhabited the Kirkstall Abbey, near where the brewery is located. The K monogram is embellished with intertwined hops (a key ingredient in Kirkstall's beers). The designs for pump clips and bottle labels use a shield device that is inspired by the main entrance window of Kirkstall Abbey. Despite the brand's historical references, the overall design is deliberately crisp and clean – the colour pallet for the brand logo is black and silver or black and white to retain a contemporary look and feel. The application is deliberately confident and fresh with the use of simple typography and supporting imagery, and strong colours – to add value and create stand out in what are generally very cluttered and busy pub environments. The beer market is full of visually complicated brewery brands and one-off beer designs that lack brand integrity. This results in confusion for the consumer and a lack of equity, in terms of building brand reputation. The new branding for Kirkstall has been designed specifically to address this issue. The key objectives of the design were to deliver provenance and build on the brewing heritage of the Kirkstall area, that was developed over the centuries. The brand is designed to deliver added value both at point of purchase and on branded merchandise. Also, budgets are limited and an important factor in the design was the ability to implement the brand cost effectively and enable range extensions to be economically applied. Ultimately, the Kirkstall brand design is about credibility, clarity and craft – and creating presence on the pub bar and retail shelf. The brand has integrity across all its applications and is immediately recognisable, helping to build a following of loyal ale drinkers.

Results: The new brand identity has delivered on all counts and has been fundamental to the brewery success. This has culminated in Kirkstall's flagship beer (Dissolution Extra IPA) winning the Sainsbury's Regional Ale award for design and quality – giving the brewery guaranteed distribution across Sainsbury's regional stores. Kirkstall Brewery saw a 166% increase in sales, 1,257% increase in profit, 320% increase in employees, 1,075% return on investment and outperformed the market by 4,154%. Profit increase was due to escalating consumer and trade demand, which coincided with the launch of the new brand.

41 FIRST & FIRST CREATIVE REAL ESTATE BRANDING | Design Firm: Fellow
Client: First & First Creative Real Estate | Designer: Will Gunderson
Creative Director: Karl Wolf | Copywriter: Eric Luoma | Account Director: Dan Peschel

Assignment: Since its inception over two years ago, First & First has operated quite successfully without a website. In some ways, the obscurity of the brand added to the lure of this growing company. First & First has quickly gained a reputation in the Twin Cities, reimagining commercial real-estate by taking historically significant sites and transforming them into inspired places of business, creativity and community. Fellow was enlisted to position and define the new First & First brand story through a variety of digital and traditional touch points.

Approach: Fellow approached the burgeoning creative real estate company's branding with simplicity in mind. A one color story was chosen to create intrigue and to emanate sophistication. First & First is also seen as a grand purveyor of fine art. Their new identity needed to be open to allow the building and the art inside to take center prominence.

Results: The work has been well received by our clients and the community.

42, 43 LA VITTORIA 2013, A UNIQUE EVENING ROOTED IN EARTHLY FLAVOURS
Design Firm: lg2boutique | Client: Johanne Demers (founder of La Vittoria)
Designers: Maude Lescarbeau, Marilyn Marois, Andrée Rouette | Print Producer: lg2fabrique
Photographer: Luc Robitaille | Copywriters: Gabrielle Godbout, Pierre Lussier
Account Executives: Marion Haimon, Sara Caradec | Account Director: Catherine Lanctôt

44, 45 TRANSFORMING AN ICONIC TOOL MANUFACTURER INTO A MULTI-INDUSTRIAL, GLOBAL GROWTH BRAND | Design Firm: Lippincott | Client: Stanley
Designers: Marc Hohmann, Sam Ayling, Imri Larsen | Strategy/Naming: Amit Sabharwal, Benjamin Grant | Strategy Director: Steve Lawrence | Production: Brendan deVallance
Photographer: David Arky (David Arky Photography) | Creative Director: Marc Hohmann

Assignment: Stanley recently expanded into industries such as security, healthcare, and oilfield services, creating the need to make a statement about who it is today – much more than a brand just for hand tools. Our challenge was to preserve Stanley's heritage as a reliable, high-quality product manufacturer, while elevating the brand into the ranks of the world's leading multi-industrial companies.

Approach: Working closely with Stanley leadership, employees and customers reinforced our belief that the positioning and visual identity must signal evolution of a unified brand with business units connected by a single concept. Cohesion was achieved with "Performance in Action," a brand essence focusing on the excellence inherent in every Stanley product, employee and business and was communicated through new positioning, tagline, architecture and messaging.

Results: The new visual identity, grounded in Stanley's heritage, simultaneously signals the brand's new direction. The new logo frees the Stanley name while maintaining the "notch" with an angular cut to the letter N in the center of the word, resulting in an arrow-like triangle that echoes the concept of action. Finally, the logo maintains the signature Stanley yellow and black palette that is synonymous with the brand.

46, 47 A NEW IDENTITY FOR THE MONTRÉAL OLYMPIC PARK
Design Firm: lg2boutique | Client: Parc Olympique | Designers: Serge Côté, Andrée Rouette
Photographer: Alain Desjean | Creative Strategist: Maryse Sauvé
Creative Directors: Claude Auchu, Serge Côté | Copywriter: Christian Letendre
Art Directors: Serge Côté, Frédéric Tremblay | Account Executive: Noémie Martin
Account Director: Catherine Lanctôt

48, 49 MERGING TWO STORIED FLAG CARRIERS TO CREATE THE PREMIER PAN-LATIN AMERICAN AIRLINE | Design Firm/Agency: Lippincott | Client: Avianca
Strategy/Naming: Allison Zeilinger, Amana Nneji | Strategy Director: Steve Lawrence
Production: Jeremy Darty, Brendan deVallance | Photographer: David Arky,
Albert Vecerka (Esto Photographics) | Designers: Rodney Abbot, Sam Ayling, Bogdan Geana, Jung Kwon | Creative Director: Rodney Abbot

Assignment: When Avianca, the flag carrier of Colombia and the oldest continuously operating airline in the Western Hemisphere, and TACA, the leading airline in Central America, merged, they asked for guidance on how best to manage the merger and brand transformation. Based on the aspiration to be the best Latin American airline, we counseled that a singular brand with a harmonized customer experience would be the most rewarding, albeit challenging, path forward – and not until those elements were aligned should the new brand be revealed.

Approach: Based on the rich heritage associated with the Avianca name in key Latin American markets, we recommended adopting the single brand name Avianca. To activate the brand, we developed brand messaging, positioning, tone of voice and brand sponsorship guidelines, as well as communications strategies and tools. Through vigorous research, we uncovered a new customer growth segment the airline would seek to attract in addition to its traditional customers. We developed a shared vision, mission, set of values and key touchpoints and created a customer experience map to guide the passenger experience.

Results: In creating the visual identity, it was important to reflect the heritage and legacy of both Avianca and TACA but also signal that this is a new, pan-Latin American Avianca. This work included a new logo, brand architecture system, livery and visual system. The new identity was built on the symbolic power of the Condor; a symbol long associated with Avianca, but now in a modern form that figuratively links South, Central and North America. We took the time – 3 years – to align internal culture and external customer experience before the new brand was revealed. The result is a unified Avianca with over 15,000 employees delivering "Latin Excellence" to more than 100 destinations. As of the official mainline brand launch, Avianca reported a record 9.7% jump in passenger demand over the first two months of the year.

50, 51 KLAUSS BOEHLER | Design Firm: lg2boutique | Client: Ango Mode
Designer: Serge Côté | Print Producer: lg2fabrique | Photographer: Alain Desjean
Creative Strategists: Stéphane Mailhiot, Marc-André Fafard | Creative Director: Serge Côté
Copywriter: Jean-François Perreault | Account Executive: Marion Haimon
Account Director: Ingrid Roussel

Assignment: Subdued, traditional and refined are the words that best describe Klauss Boehler, the British-inspired brand that creates high-end men's shirts. Refusing to compromise on quality, Klauss Boehler shirts are designed to be comfortable, durable and distinguished. The mandate was to redesign Klauss Boehler's identity to allow it to fashion an enviable place in the high-end men's shirt market. High-end fashion is a fiercely competitive market, especially for a local brands without the communication budget of its international peers. How to seduce an ever-demanding target audience? Make them feel smart and aristocratic in a world of flashy, attention-grabbing fashion. This savvy aristocrat is comfortable with the recognition from others in the know. The brand platform needed to highlight this discernment and self-assuredness.

Approach: The new Klauss Boehler branding draws its inspiration from the world of the English tailor where aesthetics, thoroughness and workmanship are bywords. The platform's graphic elements were conceived around the idea of made-to-measure, focusing on the style and refinement of the British brand's heritage.

Results: Thanks to the new identity, the brand has obtained more floor space in Hudson's Bay stores, subsequently doubling its sales figures at the retailer. The platform has also established the brand's presence across Canada while generating new business opportunities, notably with a Finnish distributor.

52, 53 CROOTS BRAND IDENTITY | Design Firm: WPA Pinfold | Client: Croots
Designer: Trudi Atkin | Typographer: Charles Stewart | Developer: Greg Kirk
Art Director: Stuart Morey | Account Director: Myles Pinfold

Assignment: The brief was to rebrand AC Supplies and reposition the company to successfully compete in the country sports and luxury goods market. The brand needed to built on its reputation for quality, craftsmanship and English heritage, and establish a communications strategy that will support growth over the forthcoming years.

Approach: We re-branded AC Supplies as Croots England - and built equity around its brand essence of authentic English craftsmanship. The name was based on the owners name and was simple, memorable and distinctive – and worked phonetically. We also developed the branding across their exclusive range of leather field sports accessories. The mark and visual language took its influence from the exquisite marquetry found on shooting rifles and the organic 'C' letterform perfectly complemented the luxury leatherwork of the company and was also ideal for embossing into the leather as a brand mark.
The design was inspired by the marquetry on shotgun barrels - leather gun bags and shooting accessories are Croots signature products. The launch of the new Croots brand was supported by a distinctive new product brochure, website (www.crootsengland.co.uk), branded products and additional point of sale. WPA Pinfold integrated the design across all media and the brand is embossed into the leather bags, to give a lasting presence. The exhibition stand build involved Croots manufacturing panels using their own facilities and materials, these panels also act as giant swatches for their leather and canvas finishes.

Results: The investment has paid dividends with unprecedented positive feedback from customers, and a brand that has added significant value and positioned Croots as market leader in the country sports accessories market – with an international reputation that is second to none. Croots saw a 35% increase in sales, and a 1,395% in return on investment.
The culmination of the success of the rebrand was when Allistair Croot personally took a telephone order from Kate Middleton.

Credits & Commentary

54, 55 IMAGES FESTIVAL 2014 | Design Firm: The Office of Gilbert Li
Client: Images Festival | Designer/Photographer: Brian Banton | Creative Director: Gilbert Li

56, 57 LOUISVILLE SLUGGER BRAND IDENTITY | Design Firm: Interbrand
Client: Hillerich & Bradsby Co. | Designers: Shane Jallick, Bart Laube
Photographers: Jeff Tilford, Katie Lipps | Chief Creative Director: Jamey Wagner
Account Manager: Will Kladakis

58, 59 MARK & GRAHAM | Design Firm: Morla Design | Client: Williams-Sonoma, Inc., Mark and Graham | Designers: Jennifer Morla, Jade Jariya | Stylist: Sara Slavin
Photographer: Sang An | Creative Director/Art Director: Jennifer Morla
Assignment: Mark and Graham is a direct-to-consumer, upscale brand, offering gifts and accessories on which a customer can make their mark with the application of unique monograms and fonts. Mark and Graham is part of Williams-Sonoma, Inc. who sought out Morla Design as its prime strategic design/business partner to handle every aspect of the launch of its new lifestyle brand.
Approach: Morla Design was brought in at the very inception of the brand by the SVP of Strategy and New Business. Work was presented directly to the CEO of Williams-Sonoma. The total time to launch the brand, with Morla Design doing all design work and customer touch-points, was nine months. Morla Design designs, produces, and creates all final art, including the every page of their retail website, all catalogs, brand copy, naming, packaging, blog, emails, and advertising, custom monograms, and product; virtually every consumer touch point.
Results: Morla Design continues to be a hands-on partner through 2014 in designing every aspect of the brand. Mark and Graham posted profits within its first year in business. This is the first time a new Williams-Sonoma brand has demonstrated profitable results within a year of launch.

60, 61 CITI BIKE (DESIGN) | Design Firm: Publicis Kaplan Thaler | Client: Citibank
Senior Designers: Tana Cieciora, Jinhee Kwon | Executive Creative Directors: Jim Kotulka, Tom Drymalski | Creative Director of Design: Roman Luba | Art Director: Nadia Kamran
Associate Creative Director of Design: Phil Arias | Chief Creative Officer: Rob Feakins

62, 63 SUMAC CAFE | Design Firm: Shadia Design | Client: Mark and Joumana Norris
Designer: Shadia Ohanessian | Sign Fabricator: It's Visual Anthony Hanna
Photographer: SlingShot Studios Steve McCawley
Assignment: A new business based on a middle eastern 'pizza' called Manouche. Name development, logo identity and branding. Applied to stationery, point of sale items, interior and exterior signage.
Approach: I presented the client with their new business name, 'Sumac Cafe - Middle Eastern Cuisine.' Sumac is one of the ingredients in Manouche. The design is full of vibrant colour, patterns and energy to match their food and culture. The cafe interiors followed through with their logo colours and a dramatic wall of Arabic letters ties the entire cafe together.
Results: Customers have been drawn to the place through its design, colour and inviting ambience. Sumac Cafe is now looking to franchise this model!

64 ARCANA BRAND BOX - MEDIUM | Design Firm: Arcana Academy
Client: Arcana Academy | Designers: Lee Walters, Alex Esseveld
Writer: Shane Hutton | Assistant: Lorene Grinberg

65 TEA AMO - SPECIALITY HEALING TEAS | Design Firm: Founded by Design
Client: Danielli's Fine Foods | Designer: Chris Thomas | Account Director: Louise Broad
Assignment: We were asked to create the brand identity, packaging and launch material for Tea Amo, a new range of healing tea blends. Our challenge was to create standout for the new brand in an already saturated market.
Approach: We designed a unique brand identity that positioned Tea Amo as an alternative to medicinal treatments. Using "healing hands" for the logo and across the whole brand language reinforced the idea of care and quality. This was combined with a unique visual style that straddled medicine and premium tea.
Results: The work resulted in a packaging range and supporting material that established Tea Amo as a serious contender in the beverage market. Stocked only in premium resellers across Sydney, the range of tea has been met with a hugely positive reaction with requests for the product to be made available in selective Sydney restaurants. It has also received interest from stockist in the USA, UK and Paris and recently featured in Entrepreneur magazine.

66 TÉLÉFILM CANADA BRANDING FOR ALL INTERNATIONAL EVENTS
Design Firm: lg2boutique | Client: Téléfilm Canada | Designer: Maude Lescarbeau
Typographer: Maude Lescarbeau | Print Producer: lg2fabrique
Creative Strategist: Pénélope Fournier | Creative Director: Claude Auchu
Copywriters: Stuart Macmillan, Éric Beaudin | Art Director: Thibault Gehard
Account Executive: Marion Haimon | Account Directors: Catherine Lanctôt, Ingrid Roussel

67 PERSPECTIVES 2014 | Design Firm: Landor Associates | Client: Landor Associates
Designers/Illustrators: Junko Maegawa, Cassia The, Stjepan Ilich, Woo Chung
Designer: Marissa Winkler | Photographer: Michael Friel | Editor: Trevor Wade
Creative Director: Paul Chock

68, 69 12E13TH ST BROCHURE | Design Firm: IF Studio
Client: DHA Capital and Continental Properties, Cantor & Pecorella, Inc.
Designers: Hisa Ide, Toshiaki Ide, John Balbarin | Design Director: Hisa Ide
Creative Director, Design Director: Toshiaki Ide | Photographers: Jacob Snavely, Kumiko Ide, Michael Imlay | Print Producer: Anya Baskin | Art Director: Kumiko Ide
Assignment: The 12 East 13th Street brochure was assigned by DHA, Continental Properties and Cantor Pecorella to market an ultra exclusive and high-end luxury condominium designed by Cetra Ruddy and located in Greenwich Village, NYC. The brochure was part of a complete graphic design and branding package for the building's marketing efforts.
Approach: It was a simple question: How can the design reflect the product? In the case of the 12 East 13th Street residence, the product is a custom designed and crafted condominium building located in a very desirable, artistic and internationally known neighborhood. Furthermore, the product is very high-end; but, we wanted to make it feel accessible to buyers through an honest approach. We designed this brochure as a "photographic sketchbook." In affect, we presented the building's craftsmanship through a still-life display of the materials. For example, pearls and flowers were photographed on the woods, marbles and steels used in kitchen and bathrooms. The neighborhood's shops, restaurants and lifestyle were captured through editorial silhouettes taken of the community's real places and objects. Further, because our firm branded the entire project, we were able to use the motif of the logo as an organizing structure in the brochure. The building's eight unique residences are represented by the logo's eight squares. We used the same squares of the logo to color code the chapters of the brochure. Thus, the brand and product of the building are seamlessly intertwined with the easily navigable structure of the brochure.
Results: The client considered the project beautifully done and well-executed. Through the design of the brochure, consumer experiences, and the high quality and feel of the residences, 12 East 13th Street was a huge success.

70, 71 DINOSAUR DESIGNS - MODERN TRIBAL | Design Firm: Hoyne
Client: Dinosaur Designs | Designers: Andrew Hoyne, Lauren Wyllie | Stylist: Meg Gray
Product Designers: Louise Olsen, Stephen Ormandy | Photographer: Nicholas Samartis
Model: Shanna Jackway | Makeup: Linda Jefferyes | Creative Director: Andrew Hoyne

72, 73 INFINITI MY14 GLOBAL BROCHURE CAMPAIGN | Design Firm: The Designory
Client: Infiniti Motors Ltd. | Designer: Matt Coonrod | Photographers: John Higginson, He & Me, Steffen Jahn | Creative Directors: Chad Weiss | Copywriters: Nic Bonilla, Abe Kwak, Stacia Jacobsen, Matt Shevin | Art Directors: Scott Izuhara, David Ly, April Larivee, Noah Huber, Paula Neff

74, 75 SOUTHCENTRE MALL SUMMER/WINTER CAMPAIGN ILLUSTRATED TYPE
Design Firm: Toolbox Design | Client: Southcentre Mall | Designer: Veronica Stark
Creative Director: Niko Potton | Copywriter: Jon Shanahan
Account Director: Aleisha Vermeulen

76 HEESEN CORPORATE BROCHURE | Design Firm: Steven Taylor Associates
Client: Heesen | Designer: Steven Taylor

77 SAINT LUCIA BROCHURE - SIMPLY BEAUTIFUL | Design Firm: Connelly Partners / ISMCP | Client: Saint Lucia Tourism Board, Nerdin St. Rose | Designers/Art Directors: Greg Wood, Matt Dugas | Production Manager: Vicki Friedman | Printer: RR Donnelly
Photographer: Stewart Ferebee | Executive Creative Director: Jonathan Plazonja
Copywriters: Sid Murlidhar, Jason Kaplan | Account Directors: JoAnne Borselli

78 WELLS FARGO LUNAR NEW YEAR CALENDAR - "ELEGANT STROKES"
Design Firm: DAE | Client: Wells Fargo | Designer/Art Director: Gigi Lam
Production Artist: San Jue | Print Producer: Frankie Lam | Junior Designer: Cindy Chu
Executive Creative Director: Sunny Teo | Agency Producer: Max Niu
Account Executive: Kelly Ko

79, 80 2014 KOMORI CALENDAR "FLAWLESS BEAUTY"
Design Firm: Toppan Printing Co., Ld. | Client: Komori Corporation
Photographer: Kate Scott | Designer: Masahiro Ogawa | Art Director: Masahiro Aoyagi

81 SOUTHWEST AIRLINES CALENDAR - "COME AWAY WITH ME" | Design Firm: DAE
Client: Southwest Airlines | Designer/Executive Creative Director: Kai Mui
Production Artists: Frankie Lam, San Jue | Art Director: Frances Chang
Agency Producer: Cindy Chu | Account Supervisor: Edward Fung

82 COKE BOTTLE CALENDAR | Design Firm: Ayşe Çelem Design | Client: Coca-Cola Turkey
Designer/Creative Director: Ayşe Çelem | Art Director: Sibel Esen | Printer: S Print

83 SAME SH*T, DIFFERENT YEAR | Design Firm: BEAMY | Client: Various
Designer/Creative Director: Ronn Lee | Copywriter: Bao Ching | Account Director: Yutien Peng

84 365 TYPOGRAPHY CALENDAR 2014 | Design Firm: Studio Hinrichs
Client: Studio Hinrichs | Designers: Kit Hinrichs, Gloria Hiek
Copywriter: Delphine Hirasuna | Printer: Blanchette Press

85 TIMBERLAND FALL 2013 CATALOG | Design Firm: Timberland In-House
Client: Timberland | Designer: Tom Yeaton | Project Manager: Lisa Rakaseder
Photographers: Thomas Hoeffgen, David Prince | Copywriter: Scott Landry

86, 87 LONG MAY SHE WAVE CATALOG | Design Firm: Studio Hinrichs
Client: Stars & Stripes Foundation | Designers: Kit Hinrichs, Dang Nguyen
Printer: Blanchette Press | Copywriter: Delphine Hirasuna
Photographers: Terry Heffernan, Kelly Powers
Assignment: Created for a touring exhibition of American Flags and Stars and Stripes Memorabilia, this catalog curates a selection of the pieces found in the collection of the Stars & Stripes Foundation. The foundation is an educational entity dedicated to conserving, restoring and chronicling the culture and history of America through the depiction of the national banner over the years.
Approach: The collection, exhibition, and book are unique in that they explore this imagery from a designer's perspective and present the flag and ephemera as a study in design iconography. We structured the catalog to reflect the collection on display and to underscore the design perspective.
Results: The catalog is sold in museum stores where the exhibition is shown, and is a popular item among flag and ephemera enthusiasts.

88 BLACK SWAN STATE THEATRE COMPANY'S 2013 SEASON CATALOGUE
Design Firm: Dessein | Client: Black Swan State Theatre Company | Designer: Esther Lee
Photographer: Robert Frith | Art Director: Geoff Bickford

89 SVA UNDERGRADUATE CATALOG 2014 | 2015 | Design Firm: Visual Arts Press, Ltd.
Client: School of Visual Arts | Designer: E. Patrick Tobin | Design Director: Michael J. Walsh
Creative Director: Anthony P. Rhodes
Assignment: Each year the School of Visual Arts creates an undergraduate catalog to present the best case for why prospective students should choose SVA, in NYC, to pursue their fine arts degree.
Approach: The original iteration of the design of the undergraduate catalog was called "Proof" – to indicate that we didn't need to use marketing gimmicks to sell prospective students a tale on why they should come to come to SVA—we just needed to present them with the facts. To do this, facts are literally spelled out about NYC and SVA in the first 60 or so pages of the catalog with images and words. We then "prove" SVA's value to an art student with the work of our students—we have more than 500 pieces of art displayed throughout the catalog.
Results: This year's catalog includes a hardcover with a lenticular image incorporating SVA's recent logo change SVA (flower) NYC. Moving the catalog allows you to see "SVA", the flower mark, or "NYC." We also chose a high-quality glossy paper stock to best show the artwork. The resulting catalog

is a substantial testament to the quality of output provided by SVA's students.

90, 91 NATIONAL GRID SECURITY AND AWARENESS CAMPAIGN
Design Firm: WPA Pinfold | Designers: Patrick Glover, Chris McMahon
Client: National Grid | Developer: Greg Kirk | Creative Director: Richard Hurst
Animator: John Bell

92 MARCH 2014 COVER | Design Firm: GQ | Client: GQ
Designer: Chelsea Cardinal | Design Director: Fred Woodward

93 CONFESSIONS OF A DRONE WARRIOR Design Firm: GQ | Client: GQ
Designer: Benjamin Bours | Design Director: Fred Woodward

93 THE LUCKIEST VILLAGE IN THE WORLD | Design Firm: GQ | Client: GQ
Designer: Andre Jointe | Design Director: Fred Woodward

94 THE TRUCK STOP KILLER | Design Firm: GQ | Client: GQ
Designer: Benjamin Bours | Design Director: Fred Woodward

94 THE SWEAR JAR | Design Firm: GQ | Client: GQ
Designer: Benjamin Bours | Design Director: Fred Woodward

95 LOVE SEX & MADNESS | Design Firm: GQ | Client: GQ
Designer: Chelsea Cardinal | Design Director: Fred Woodward

96 BOOB JOB | Design Firm: GQ | Client: GQ
Designer: Chelsea Cardinal | Design Director: Fred Woodward

96 4TH & FOREVER | Design Firm: GQ | Client: GQ
Designer: Andre Jointe | Design Director: Fred Woodward

97 NATURAL BORN KILLERS | Design Firm: GQ | Client: GQ
Designer: Benjamin Bours | Design Director: Fred Woodward

97 OOPS YOU JUST HIRED THE WRONG HIT MAN | Design Firm: GQ | Client: GQ
Designer: John Muñoz | Design Director: Fred Woodward

98 MEN OF THE YEAR 2013 | Design Firm: GQ | Client: GQ
Designer: Chelsea Cardinal | Design Director: Fred Woodward

98 CLOUDY WITH A CHANCE OF STINGING NETTLE FLAN AND TOMATO COULIS
Design Firm: GQ | Client: GQ | Designer: Chelsea Cardinal | Design Director: Fred Woodward

99 EVERYONE'S A COMEDIAN | Design Firm: GQ | Client: GQ
Designer: Andre Jointe | Design Director: Fred Woodward

100, 101 WORLD WILDLIFE FUND WINTER 2013 | Design Firm: Pentagram
Client: World Wildlife Fund | Designer: Carla Delgado | Art Director: DJ Stout
Assignment: The Winter 2013 issue of World Wildlife magazine, the official publication of the World Wildlife Fund based in Washington DC, was the launch issue of the new title created by Pentagram Austin. The unique cover format always features a macro-image of an animal's hide, skin, or fur and when the reader turns to the first spread in the magazine the corresponding species and its conservation story are revealed.
Approach: We designed a cover format to give WWF magazine a unique identity.
Results: The magazine has performed well and is popular with the membership.

102, 103 WORLD WILDLIFE FUND SPRING 2014 ISSUE | Design Firm: Pentagram
Client: World Wildlife Fund | Designer: Carla Delgado | Art Director: DJ Stout
Assignment: The Spring 2014 issue of World Wildlife magazine, the official publication of the World Wildlife Fund based in Washington DC, was the second issue of the new title created by Pentagram Austin. The unique cover format always features a macro-image of an animal's hide, skin, or fur and when the reader turns to the first spread in the magazine the corresponding species and its conservation story are revealed.
Approach: We designed a cover that gives WWF magazine a unique identity.
Results: The magazine has performed well and is popular with the membership.

104-106 FSHNUNLIMITED MAGAZINE (F.U.) | Design Firm: Faith
Client: fshnunlimited magazine | Designer/Creative Director: Paul Sych
Typographer: Paul Sych | Photographers: Alexander Eros Rocco, Mike Ruiz, Hanna Sider, Vicky Lam, Regen Chen, Arline Malakian | Illustrator: Sarah Clifford Rashotte
Assignment: Fshnunlimited magazine was created as a vehicle to discover, explore and exhibit influential Canadian talent. At its core, the magazine aims to provide a stage for talented local artists to gain exposure and reverence in an industry that is difficult to shine in. Spearheaded by a collective of fashion photographers, artists and writers, Fshnunlimited aspires to deliver a renewed Canadian voice to the international arena.
Approach: Fshnunlimited was founded by me, Paul Sych. As the Creative Director of the magazine, I solicited and assembled talent that helped mold the voice of the magazine and mirrored what I envisioned it to become. Fshnunlimited embodies a unique visual language. The pacing of the magazine is both rhythmic and esoteric, drawing upon striking graphical cues to animate the intention of the written pieces, contemporary art, and editorial features. This visceral voice is personified in the typography, layout, and cover designs of each issue; created intuitively as a response to the work featured. They reflect the nature of the magazine and its reverence of art.
Results: Fshnunlimited is the antithesis to the traditional, mainstream fashion publication. We celebrate the culture of creation through incredible people and remarkable work – providing a voice for the identity, intelligence, and design behind fashion and art. Our magazine is intended to reach the individual looking beyond the mundane, regurgitated content that magazine culture is so often subjected to – someone who would like to experience Canadian fashion on a refreshing level. The reaction to Fshnunlimited has been supportive, positive and encouraging – lauding the magazine's mandate to combine fashion and art under a Canadian lens that is rarely praised. People seem genuinely engaged by the magazine's unique content and brash visuals. Many have said to me that "it is about time" something like this has come along in our industry.

107 AS IF ISSUE 4 COVER GRETA GERWIG | Company: AS IF Media Group, LLC
Client: AS IF Magazine | Designer: Daniel Irizarry | Photographer: Tatijana Shoan
Production Manager: Scott Fishkind | Art Directors: Tatijana Shoan, Scott Fishkind

108 CLOSE-UP Company: AS IF Media Group, LLC | Client: AS IF Magazine
Photographer: Tatijana Shoan | Designer: Diego Pinilla | Art Producer: Chuck Close

108, 109 CIGARETTES AND LEGS | Company: AS IF Media Group, LLC
Client: AS IF Magazine | Production Manager: Scott Fishkind | Art Director: Tatijana Shoan
Photographers: Robert Whitman, Tatijana Shoan | Designer: Nathan Braceros

109 TWENTY FIRST CENTURY MUSE | Company: AS IF Media Group, LLC
Client: AS IF Magazine | Production Manager: Scott Fishkind
Photographer: Bert Stern | Designer: Carla Miller

110 224PLUS / 225PLUS - CUSTOMER MAGAZINE | Design Firm: Peter Schmidt Group
Client: Sal. Oppenheim jr. & Cie. | Creative Director/Designer: Bernd Vollmöller
Designers: Gerrit Hinkelbein

111 WAYWARD ARTS MAGAZINE | Design Firm: Underline Studio
Client: Flash Reproductions Ltd., Underline Studio
Designers/Creative Directors: Claire Dawson, Fidel Peña | Writers: Stuart Ross, Rob Duncan, Doug Dolan, Scott McLeod | Printer: Flash Reproductions Ltd.
Photographers: Colin Faulkner, Paul Weeks, Daniel Ehrenworth, Angus Fergusson, Joanne Ratajczak, Shanghoon, Luis Albuquerque
Illustrators: Graham Roumieu, Ben Weeks, Prashant Miranda

112, 113 S MAGAZINE NO15 | Design Firm: Piera Wolf | Client: S Magazine
Designer: Piera Wolf | Agency: S Magazine | Editor-in-Chief: Jens Stoltze
Creative Director: Christina Chin | Art Director: Ferdinando Verderi
Managing Editor: Mazy Brujjerdi | Photography Editor: Mads Teglers
Assistant Designer: Emmelie Franzén | Assistant Art Director: Margot Populaire
Contributing Editor: Stefanie Djie | Digital Director: Emilia Isaksson
Online Editor: Emil S. Nissen | Contributors: 223, Aliya Naumoff, Bill Powers, Charlie Engman, David Shama, David Standish, Eddie Chacon, Fabiola Zamora, Ferdinando Verderi, Jesse Leitinen, Johan Alfsson, Kendall Frémont, Lars Botten, Lina Scheynius, Lynne Larsen, M. Sharkey, Mads Teglers, Magnus Reed, Mario de Armas, Marton Perlaki, Massimo Leardini, Nick Haramis, Ole Marius Fossen, Philip Leff, Pejman Biroun Vand, Roman Goebels, Stoltze & Stefanie | Cover Photographer: Stoltze & Stefanie | Model: Joséphine de la Baume
Dress: Thom Browne | Fur: Adrienne Landau
Assignment: "S" is a deluxe, biannual art and fashion magazine based in Copenhagen and New York, focused on the human form and human condition. Since its first issue nine years ago, "S" has been committed to stunning fashion photography, boundary-pushing visual art and design, and thoughtprovoking feature articles, giving freedom for some of the most original and intriguing creative talents of our time to express their unique visions.
Approach: Every single issue of S Magazine has its own voice. The design of this current issue No15 is inspired by the grid system of Jan Tschichold. This concept is being applied throughout the magazine and executed in an original way. The goal was to intrigue, tease, make curious. We approached this by playing with fragmented type and imagery in order to reflect the theme of S Magazine and the nature of the stunningly aesthetic and intriguing imagery.
Results: The connective theme of the new issue, "S" 15, is "time." In this "real-time" age where things seem to happen ever more frequently and at ever greater velocity, this issue of "S" has the effect of slowing time down for each reader who opens it, with 304 pages (320 in the Danish edition) that beguile, mesmerize and entrance. Pages that make you forget to turn the page With featured talents such as Joséphine de la Baume, Edward Leida, Sagmeister & Walsh, Asger & Troels Carlsen among others. "S" 15 lets its readers escape the rush of the mad world around them and rediscover some of the time they'd lost track of.

114 LOYOLA MARYMOUNT UNIVERSITY PUBLICATION | Design Firm: Pentagram
Client: Loyola Marymount University | Designer: Barrett Fry | Art Director: DJ Stout

115 REBEL, REBEL | Design Firm: 9 Threads | Client: Footwear Plus magazine
Designers/Creative Directors: Trevett McCandliss, Nancy Campbell | Stylist: Kim Johnson
Photographer: Trevett McCandliss | Fashion Director: Angela Velasquez
Art Director: Tim Jones
Assignment: Feature fall fashion inspired by the '90s grunge movement.
Approach: For this story featuring grunge-inspired fashion, we used a combination of blackletter characters with hand-constructed characters. The constructed type contains blackletter and art deco elements.

116 ALL CREATURES GREAT AND SMALL | Design Firm: 9 Threads
Client: Earnshaw's magazine | Designers/Creative Directors: Trevett McCandliss, Nancy Campbell | Art Director: Tim Jones | Photographer: Cleo Sullivan
Fashion Director: Angela Velasquez | Stylist: Michel Onofrio

117 ART GALLERY OF MISSISSAUGA SIGNAGE | Design Firm: The White Room Inc
Client: Art Gallery of Mississauga | Designer: Neil Rodman

118, 119 NPR HEADQUARTERS AND PRODUCTION STUDIOS
Design Firm: Poulin + Morris Inc. | Client: NPR | Designers: Ani Ardzivian, Erik Herter
Design Director: Richard Poulin | Agency: Poulin + Morris Inc.
Assignment: NPR was in need of an environmental graphics and wayfinding sign program after relocating to a 440,000-square-foot, state-of-the-art, LEED-Gold certified headquarters in Washington, DC.
Approach: A comprehensive environmental graphics, donor recognition, and wayfinding sign program was developed for NPR's new headquarters illustrating the history of the organization—from its beginnings in radio to its current involvement in video, apps, and photojournalism. A 52-foot-tall, LED-illuminated tower made of steel and glass, reminiscent of a radio tower, identifies the building. LED lighting pulsing through the vertical icon tower, referencing radio waves, culminates at a large-scale NPR logotype. An LED "ticker" ribbon set above the entrance wraps around the building displaying headlines culled from NPR data feeds. The building's main lobby features a 2-story-high, digital "media mosaic" composed of LED screens displaying NPR programming, news headlines, and member station information from the NPR website, news, and music apps. NPR's mission statement runs along the lobby walls, creating a sense of motion—a visually dynamic effect used throughout the building.
Results: Poulin + Morris continued to work with NPR on a variety of projects for their new headquarters, including a permanent, interactive lobby exhibition entitled "This is NPR," and branding and identity programs for the NPR

store—NPR Commons and their staff cafeteria—Soundbites Café.

120, 121 "THE KOGANEI" ENVIRONMENTAL GRAPHIC DESIGN PROJECT OF KOGANEI CIVIC CENTER | Design Firm: KMD Inc. | Client: Koganei-shi, City Office
Designers: Kei Miyazaki, Hideaki Tomita

Assignment: This is a public facility, which has several functions such as large and small halls, lecture rooms, a gallery, etc. We are requested to introduce "something like Koganei city" into this building.

Approach: We expressed shapes of park, river and spring water as a concrete form in the building based on the geographical features of Koganei city, filled with lush greenery and streams. A stage curtain for the main hall was also designed by us as one of the space components of the building. We selected "roads of Koganei city" for the design motif.

Results: People are comfortable with the roads and greenery in this facility. Their identity within the city is reflected in the building, through original design, which is different from other common facilities.

122, 123 SIEC SIGNAGE | Design Firm: Parallax Design
Client: Department of Further Education, Employment, Science and Technology
Designers: Matthew Remphrey, Andrew Smart

Assignment: The Sustainable Industries Education Centre (SIEC) is a $120m redevelopment of an unused Mitsubishi automotive assembly line in the Adelaide suburb of Tonsley. A major tenant of the centre was to be the state's largest provider of vocational education and training, TafeSA. TafeSA intended to relocate all of its construction trades to SIEC. Parallax was commissioned to develop a comprehensive signage system allowing staff, students and visitors to navigate five buildings (inserted into the existing building) across four levels and open workshops — some 45,000m2 in total.

Approach: The architectural approach to refurbishing the existing building was to present it honestly, with all materials and services visible. The very building became a teaching aid. A recurring motif was the use of fins in varying size, spacing and materials, which produce a moire effect on the light. We used these fins for graphics that can be seen from one direction and hidden from another view, and perforated aluminium to create a moire pattern effect the viewer experiences when they move past, over and under the signs. The shear scale of the building was another consideration. Down the main "street" connecting entrances and bisecting buildings and workshop, we designed a series of 7m high perforated navigational totems. The totems are completely self-supporting with no internal structure, and possess a lightness that belies their size. We were also responsible for developing a strategy that named buildings, located rooms, indicated pedestrian and vehicular movement in the open workshops, and took into account PPE, HAZMAT and emergency signage requirements.

Results: SIEC and TafeSA opened in January 2014. The signage system has been so well retrieved, TafeSA intends to roll it out to all of its other campuses.

124, 125 BRIC HOUSE | Design Firm: Poulin + Morris Inc. | Client: BRIC
Designer: Andreina Carrillo | Design Director: Richard Poulin

126, 127 HYATT REGENCY HOTEL, NEW ORLEANS WAYFINDING SYSTEM
Design Firm: Lorenc+Yoo Design Inc | Client: Hyatt Regency, New Orleans, LA.
Designers: Jan Lorenc, Chung Yoo, Mac Liu

Assignment: Hyatt Regency New Orleans recently underwent a $200,000,000 expansion program, which placed the front door where the back door had been, and hired a sign vendor to redo the signage. The problem was that the inherent issues that existed with the original hotel were complicated by the much more complex expansion. Lorenc+Yoo Design was asked to redesign and rethink the present program which was in place for only 6 months.

Approach: Our task was to analyze the hotel and convention center and to ease the wayfinding issues by having the wayfinding direct from node to node and to smaller sections once you arrived at that node. Our task was to simplify the nomenclature by recommending a simpler naming structure for the hotels components, by defining the areas of the nodes so that clarity of spaces existed, and by assisting in wayfinding concerns at decision points. In the lobby our task was to get the guests to their rooms which was a complex journey.

Results: We provided signage in major decision points. The signage program had to be much more defined and bold in the spaces as opposed to a background element with too much information. Effective signage for complex environments reflect well on the facility, and guests without bad wayfinding experiences are more likely to return.

128 "FLYING KITE" SIGNAGE DESIGN FOR TAIWAN HAKKA CULTURAL CENTER
Design Firm: KMD Inc. | Client: Council for Hakka Affairs
Designers: Kei Miyazaki, Natsuko Hosokawa

129 TANGERINE INTERIORS | Design Firm: Concrete Design Communications
Client: Tangerine (formerly ING Direct) | Designers: Ryan Crouchman, Jonathon Yule
Creative Directors: Diti Katona, John Pylypczak

130, 131 ROSEWOOD LONDON ENVIRONMENTAL SIGNAGE PROGRAM
Design Firm: Regina Rubino / Robert Louey | Client: Regina Rubino / Robert Louey
Designers: Regina Rubino, Christy Thrasher | Design Director: Regina Rubino
Chief Creative Officer: Robert Louey

132, 133 NOVO NORDISK NORTH AMERICAN HEADQUARTERS
Design Firm: Poulin + Morris Inc. | Client: Granum A/I | Designers: Andreina Carrillo, Erik Herter
Design Director: Richard Poulin

134, 135 FROM PENCIL TO PIXEL | Design Firm/Agency: Lippincott
Client: Monotype | Designers: Rodney Abbot, Jung Kwon, Chet Purtilar, Andrew Chiu, Leonor Mondes de Oca | Creative Directors: Rodney Abbot, Fabian Diaz, Heather Stern
Photographer: Albert Vecerka (Esto Photographics)

Assignment: We partnered with Monotype to bring the New York edition of "Pencil to Pixel" to life by creating two distinct yet connected experiences of historical and modern typeface design. The goal was an exhibit that was definitively New York, but could be translated into an ongoing series from city to city.

Approach: Eliminating graphic devices and color allowed for typefaces to take

center stage as visitors explored the space. The exhibit's two rooms, "Pencil" and "Pixel," each had an immersive experience telling Monotype's brand story and displaying its extensive portfolio. "Pencil" contained original hand drawings for hot-metal faces, hand-cut films, production drawings for Times New Roman commissioned for The Times of London, concept art, photos, publications, and metal and film master art. "Pixel" included cutting-edge digital applications, the first bitmap designs and a digital Tagboard aggregating social conversation around the event in real-time.

Results: By infusing macro and micro typography that were both static and dynamic, we told a cohesive story of how type plays a role in shaping the art of communication. The show drew thousands of visitors during the week, offering designers and non-designers alike a new appreciation for the craft of typography.

136, 137 EATON EXPERIENCE CENTER | Design Firm: Ralph Appelbaum Associates
Client: Eaton | Designer: Ralph Appelbaum Associates
Project Director/Lead Designer: Tim Ventimiglia | Exhibition Designer: Katherine Kline
Project Manager/Senior Designer: Walter Froetscher | Executive Producer: Alex Vlack
Writer/Content Developer: Darla Decker | Content Coordinator: Heather Christian Smith
Graphic Designers: Mia Beurskens, Michael Schnepf, Robert Homack
Senior Producer: Lilly Preston | Interactive Designer: Nina Boesch
Project Coordinator: Carlin Wragg | Senior Developers: Michael Neault, Alex Nguyen
Animators: Andrew Papa, Jamie Boud | Lead Architects: Pickard Chilton Architects Lead Architects | Architects of Record: KA Architecture, Design Architects of Record
LED Mesh: Traxon Industries Inc. | General Contractor: A.M. Higley Company
Lighting Design: Cline Bettridge Bernstein Lighting Design Inc.
Steel Fabrication: Engineered Products Inc. | Inlaid Stone Floor: Creative Edge Inc.
Lenticular Graphics: Softmotion 3D | Overall AV Integration: Electrosonic UK
Structural Engineering: Shenberger & Associates Inc | Photographer: Chuck Choi
Electrical Engineering: Karpinski Engineering Inc.

Assignment: Eaton Experience Center is a large-scale immersive multimedia installation integrated into the main atrium space of Eaton Center. The EEC was created to help communicate Eaton's values and strengths to employees; customers; suppliers; business partners; media; and government and civic leaders and to provide a communal space for employee and talent acquisition events. The installation consists of an Entry Gallery with large-scale lenticular graphics, an atrium space with an 80 foot long LED mesh Curtain that features abstract or natural landscapes and data visualizations, a brilliant 53-foot LED Chandelier suspended from the ceiling, an immersive soundscape, and four large interactive multi-touch screens.

Approach: The design solutions varied based on the purpose assigned to each area. Our design solution for the Entry Gallery was to use large-scale lenticular graphics that showcase Eaton solutions - letting them visibly emerge through an analogue interactive. Our design solution for the atrium included various digital media surfaces. Digital animations produced for the Chandelier and Curtain explained -- mostly without words -- Eaton's various markets and solutions, while the four touch-screen media tables introduced world trends and needs that indicate future growth areas for power management. As specific technologies and solutions change rapidly, it was important to keep the content at a very high level and speak to overarching themes and trends in a way that is accessible, engaging, visionary, and at times even poetic.

Results: Although the majority of users are Eaton employees, Eaton Center hosts visitors on a daily basis. The design served to inspire and inform both employees and visitors of the importance of Eaton's activities on a daily basis. As Eaton CEO Sandy Cutler described, shortly after the grand opening, "Every morning when I drive up Eaton Boulevard and make the graceful turn into our entrance, I see the power of Eaton – our values and our culture visually playing out in this site… the bright pulsing blue emanating from our Customer Experience Center and Chandelier – the veritable power that comes from our customers that energizes our entire company."

138 SHOP/SHOW | Design Firm: Risd Class of 2013
Client: Risd Class of 2013 | Designer: Wael Morcos

139 MECHANICAL BEE INTEGRATION #4 | Design Firm: IDEAS360° | SG360° a Segerdahl company | Designer/Illustrator: Michael Pantuso
Executive Creative Director/Illustrator/Designer: Michael Pantuso

Approach: Mechanical Bee Integration is the first in the "Mechanical Integration Series," which is still in progress. Mechanical Integrations begin with minimal planning, preliminary sketches, or reference. They start with an idea either inspired or imagined. The design process is approached in such a way to be unencumbered by the influences of plans or pre-conceived outcomes. Each vector-based illustration is created and developed in much the same way as building a collage or abstract design. Elements are added, moved around, and positioned into the overall composition. Using Adobe Illustrator CS6, elements are created one at a time and layered accordingly. The final result or destination is unknown. Consequently, there are no final versions. Only version numbers.

140 MECHANICAL SQUID INTEGRATION #8
Design Firm: IDEAS360° | SG360° a Segerdahl company
Executive Creative Director/Illustrator/Designer: Michael Pantuso

Approach: Mechanical Squid Integration is the second in the "Mechanical Integration Series," which is still in progress. Mechanical Integrations begin with minimal planning, preliminary sketches, or reference. They start with an idea, inspired or imagined. The design process is approached in such a way to be unencumbered by the influences of plans or pre-conceived outcomes. Each vector-based illustration is created and developed in the same way as building a collage or abstract design. Elements are added, moved around, and positioned into the overall composition. Built using Adobe Illustrator CS6, elements are created one at a time and layered accordingly. The final result or destination is unknown. Consequently, there are no final versions. Only version numbers.

141 THE WALKING DEAD COMIC PRINT | Design Firm: INNOCEAN USA
Client: Hyundai Motor America | Designer: Arnie Presiado | Print Producer: Michelle South

Credits & Commentary

Executive Creative Director: Greg Braun | Creative Directors: Scott Muckenthaler, Tom Pettus, Barney Goldberg | Copywriter: Jeb Quaid | Account Executive: Nadia Hernandez
Account Director: Juli Swingle

142 SOMNAMBULISTS | Design Firm: University of Wisconsin—Green Bay
Designer: Kristy Deetz

143 THE WALKING DEAD CHOP SHOP JOURNAL | Design Firm: INNOCEAN USA
Client: Hyundai Motor America | Designer: Derek Arzoo | Print Producer: Michelle South
Executive Creative Director: Greg Braun | Creative Directors: Tom Pettus, Barney Goldberg, Scott Muckenthaler | Copywriter: Brian Chin | Art Producer: Kristen Miller
Art Director: Charles Gerstner | Art Buyer: Barb Sanson
Account Executive: Nadia Hernandez | Account Director: Juli Swingle

144 MASON ZIMBLER WEBSITE | Design Firm: Mason Zimbler | Client: Mason Zimbler
Designers: Ivan Najera, Bryan Miles | Developers: Stefan von Ellenrieder, Anthony Nguyen,
Rob Lowe, Iwona Just | Creative Directors: Jeffrey Neely, Henry Medrano, Alan Kittle
Copywriters: Lauren Reichman, Lori Otto, Monica Cardenas
Associate Creative Directors: Andrew Womack, Andrei Cervantes, Kathy Horn
Art Director: Jimmy Dyer
Assignment: Mason Zimbler is an integrated agency rooted in the digital world. We recently refreshed our brand, so we needed a new website to reflect our expertise and serve as a showcase for our work and personality.
Approach: As the primary presence of our brand online, the site is designed to live and breathe, with content tiles that can be updated as new work is developed. The colorful tiles represent all types of site content, including leadership profiles, portfolio pieces and client partners. Smaller tiles pull in social media feeds from Twitter and Instagram. The only spaces in the field of tiles fill in with teasers to case studies as you scroll, demonstrating how we combine creative and technology to tell a client's story, filling in any "gaps" in their marketing spectrum. The primary audience for the site is potential clients, so the content is very focused on the work we do and how well it has worked for previous clients. A blog and news section are updated regularly to demonstrate thought leadership in the space.

145 UA CHINA EXPERIENCE | Design Firm: HUSH Studios
Client: Under Armour | Designers: Bryan Louie, Erik Yang, Ben Gray, Carlos Ancalmo,
Goran Krstic, Christina Hogan, Andre Salyer, Wes Louie
Project Coordinator: Katherine Conaway | Producers: Eric Alba, Sue McNamara, Barry Gilbert
Creative Director: Jodi Terwilliger | Executive Creative Directors: David Schwarz, Erik Karasyk
Editor: John McSwain | Architect: Marc Thorpe Design | Animators: Pedro Sanches, Carl Burton, Emmett Dzieza, Eric Concepcion, Ross McCampbell, Matt Hanson, James Zanoni
Other: ANTFOOD, Audio Visual & Controls Inc.

146 ERIN TRACY BRIDAL & FINE JEWELLERY | Design Firm: The White Room Inc.
Client: Erin Tracy | Designer: Karolina Loboda | Stylist: Cory Ng | Art Director: Karolina Loboda
Photographer: Felix Wong | Hair/Makeup: Susana Hong

147 WALLACE CHURCH TUNA PARTY INVITE: FORTUNE FISH
Design Firm: Wallace Church, Inc | Client: Wallace Church, Inc | Designer: Stan Church

148 FIRST & FIRST CREATIVE REAL ESTATE BRANDING | Design Firm: Fellow
Client: First & First Creative Real Estate | Designer: Will Gunderson
Creative Director: Karl Wolf | Copywriter: Eric Luoma | Account Director: Dan Peschel
Assignment: Since its inception over two years ago, First & First has operated quite successfully without a website. In some ways, the obscurity of the brand added to the lure of this growing company. First & First has quickly gained a reputation in the Twin Cities, reimagining commercial real-estate by taking historically significant sites and transforming them into inspired places of business, creativity and community. Fellow was enlisted to position and define the new First & First brand story through a variety of digital and traditional touch points.
Approach: Fellow approached the burgeoning creative real estate company's branding with simplicity in mind. A one color story was chosen to create intrigue and to emanate sophistication. First & First is also seen as a grand purveyor of fine art. Their new identity needed to be open to allow the building and the art inside to take center prominence.
Results: The work was well received by our clients and the community.

149 BRAND CREATION | Design Firm: Monogram | Client: History Will Be Kind
Creative Director: Amy Nadaskay | Designer: Lauren Haire

150 OLD OX BREWERY LOGO (TOP) | Design Firm: Peppermill Projects
Client: Old Ox Brewery | Designer: Hannah Peterson
Chief Creative Director: Jennifer Culpepper
Assignment: Our challenge was to create a strong and memorable logo to help a new, local brewery stand out in a wildly creative industry.
Approach: During our brand discovery, Peppermill Projects developed the personification of the old ox, a retired farmer turned brewmaster. After a long life of hard work and hard living, Old Ox has transferred his passion for farming to beer-making. With the determination and steadfastness of an old ox, he never settles for less than perfection. That's what makes his beer so good.
Results: After developing this personality, we designed a logo that was bold with a hint of vintage farm iconography. We added horns to this hand-lettered, typographic solution to create the ox head and form a cohesive mark.

150 ANGELS & COWBOYS WINE LABEL (BOTTOM)
Design Firm: Michael Schwab Studio | Clients: Angels & Cowboys, Yoav Gilat
Designer: Michael Schwab
Assignment: To create a unique wine label
Approach: Pairing the delicacy of angels with the rugged strength of cowboys.
Results: Graphically alluring design + delicious wine = success.

151 25 FRAMES | Design Firm: The Partners
Client: Film and Video Umbrella | Designer: Nick Eagleton

152 GOOGLE NEW YORK - NEON (TOP) | Design Firm: Graham Hanson Design
Client: Google New York | Designer: Graham Hanson
Assignment: Identify Google's New York headquarters.
Approach: Integration of both Google and New York.
Results: Google's dynamic identity, as per their doodles, provides latitude for

a wide range of solutions. Our solution adopted a single letter from each of six iconic NY landmarks signs (Domino Sugar, Pepsi, Tower Records, etc.) to form the Google name in a monumental neon scale.

152 GOOGLE LOGO (BOTTOM) | Design Firm: The Rivalry | Client: Google
Client Support: Google UXA | Designer: Jesse Kaczmarek

153 GOOGLE PRODUCT ICONS | Design Firm: The Rivalry | Client: Google
Designer: Jesse Kaczmarek | Production: Google Art Dept.
Client Support: Google Creative Lab

154 TUCKERS TAVERN LOGO | Design Firm: Shamlian Creative | Client: Marty Grims
Designers: Karen Wainwright, Joshua Phillips | Creative Director: Fred Shamlian

155 TENNIS COMPETITION LOGO (1ST) | Design Firm: Odear | Client: Odear Open
Designers: Thomas Palmbäck, Karl-Magnus Boske

155 FICKS COCKTAIL FORTIFIER LOGO (2ND) | Design Firm: Liquid Agency
Client: Ficks | Designers: Jesse Amborn, Jay Cech | Creative Director: Brian Dixon

155 DIGITAL ARTS LOGO (3RD) | Design Firm: Mermaid, Inc. | Client: digital arts
Designer: Sharon McLaughlin

155 TENTH AND PAGE REALTY LOGO (4TH) | Design Firm: The General Design Co.
Client: Tenth and Page Realty | Designer: Carrie Brickell | Art Director: Soung Wiser

155 NEW ZEALAND OPERA (5TH) | Design Firm: Alt Group
Client: New Zealand Opera | Designer: Dean Poole

155 LA.B MONOGRAM (6TH) | Design Firm: Design is Play | Client: Los Angeles Boulders
Designers: Mark Fox, Angie Wang | Hand Lettering: Mark Fox

156 NEBRASKA ANTIQUE FARMING ASSOCIATION LOGO (TOP)
Design Firm: Bailey Lauerman | Client: Nebraska Antique Farming Association
Designer: Brandon Oltman | Creative Director: Ron Sack
Assignment: Design a logo for the Nebraska Antique Farming Association, whose mission is dedicated to the promotion and preservation of farm machinery.
Approach: Our inspiration came from studying various vintage farm implements. The tractor rules the farm and so we decided to use the old cast iron tractor seats as the basis for our logo. Quite often the tractor seats were designed to promote the manufacturer's name in the seat. We designed ours to do the same in promoting the Nebraska Antique Farming Association.
Results: The association is finding ways to infuse the logo on other brand and promotional materials. We hope to create actual cast iron seats out of this logo.

156 YUMBLEBEE LOGO (BOTTOM) | Design Firm: Squires & Company
Client: Yumblebee | Designer: Ryan Bailey | Creative Director: Geoff German
Assignment: Design a logo for Yumblebee, a start-up social network for foodies, that would garner attention among foodies and financial backing from investors.
Approach: Yumblebee is all about food, fun, and simplicity. Our objective was to capture that essence and communicate it through the illustration of a "bee", as pronounced in the logo. The body and stinger of the bee create a speech bubble shape, reinforcing that Yumblebee is a social network for foodies.
Results: The logo was well received by the client and was instrumental in garnering attention for the social network among investors and users alike.

157 MAPR TECHNOLOGIES ELEPHANT (1ST) | Design Firm: Craig-Teerlink Design
Client: MapR Technologies | Designer/ Creative Director: Jean Craig-Teerlink

157 DOGPATCH BOULDERS (2ND) | Design Firm: Design is Play
Client: Touchstone Climbing | Designers: Mark Fox, Angie Wang | Illustrator: Mark Fox

157 SUNDANCE CONSTRUCTION LOGO (3RD) | Design Firm: Hawkeye Communications
Client: Sundance Construction | Designer: Alfonso Ramos
Creative Director: Terry McCoy | Art Director: Justin McCoy

157 PALMIERI BROS PAVING (4TH) | Design Firm: AG Creative
Client: Palmieri Bros Paving | Designer: Stewart Jung | Account Director: Virginia Mouland

157 SISTERS LOGO (5TH) | Design Firm: Leynivopnid | Client: Sisters
Designers: Einar Gylfason, Unnur Valdis | Art Director: Einar Gylfason

158 ANTHONY GISMONDI IDENTITY (TOP) | Design Firm: Toolbox Design
Client: Anthony Gismondi | Designer: Veronica Stark
Creative Director: Niko Potton | Account Director: Kala Mackay

158 ROYAL VOLUME LOGO (BOTTOM) | Design Firm: HOOK
Client: Royal Volume | Designer: Brady Waggoner

159 EVENT ACADEMY LOGO (1ST) | Design Firm: Flake | Client: Event Academy
Designer: Eero Heikkinen | Illustrator: Janne Uotila

159 A TRIP TO THE MOON (2ND) | Design Firm: H.Tuncay Design
Client: "A Trip to the Moon" Film and Production Company | Designer: Haluk Tuncay

159 PEET'S COFFEE & TEA LOGO DESIGN (3RD) | Design Firm: Michael Schwab Studio
Client: Peet's Coffee & Tea | Designer: Michael Schwab Studio Elixir Design
Creative Director: Karin Bryant

159 CAFFE AFICIONADO (4TH) | Design Firm: The General Design Co.
Client: Caffe Aficionado | Designer: Caroline Brickell | Art Director: Soung Wiser

159 RED BRACER (5TH) | Design Firm: H.Tuncay Design
Client: "Red Bracer"production company | Designer: Haluk Tuncay

160 ROSE COLE (1ST) | Design Firm: Chase Design Group | Client: Rose Cole
Designer: Evangeline Joo | Creative Director: Margo Chase
Associate Creative Director: Paula Hansanugrum

160 KESTREL AIRCRAFT LOGO (2ND) | Design Firm: Leap | Client: Kestrel Aircraft
Designers: Aaron Scott, Jeff Monahan

160 CREEK SHOW LOGO (3RD) | Design Firm: Pentagram
Client: Waller Creek Revitalization Initiative | Designer: Barrett Fry
Illustrator: Marc Burckhardt | Art Director: DJ Stout

160 ARCHITECTURAL FIRM LOGO (4TH) | Design Firm: mkcreative
Client: Turett Architect | Designer: Michelle Kang

160 LOGO DENTAL CLINIC BLANCO RAMOS (5TH) | Design Firm: xose teiga, studio.
Client: Clinic Blanco Ramos | Designer/Creative Director/Art Director: Xose Teiga

Credits & Commentary

161 POINT STATE PARK/GREAT ALLEGHENY PASSAGE MEDALLION
Design Firm: Landesberg Design | Client: Allegheny Trail Alliance
Designers: Joe Petrina, Kipp Madison, Rick Landesberg | Art Director: Rick Landesberg

Assignment: We were asked to conceive a public moment that marks the confluence of Pittsburgh's three rivers within Point State Park; It had to 1) imply a sense of The Point's historical importance (in the mid-18th century it was one of the most strategic places in the world); and 2) signal the terminus of the just-completed Great Allegheny Passage bike trail from Washington DC to Pittsburgh. There was a need to have that particular spot where people say, "Let's take the photo here."

Approach: The site, owned by Pennsylvania's Department of Conservation and Natural Resources, receives heavy usage. Known as The Point, it is the confluence of three rivers, and is the ground zero spot of the entire region. It sits within the just-restored Point State Park, itself a landmark of landscape architecture and urban park design. In the 18th century, Native American French, and British cultures - each with their own aspirations - collided here. In coordination with our client at the Allegheny Trail Alliance, we devised a contemporary bronze medallion that suggests (but does not attempt to define) the importance of the place. Within the plaque are the outlines of the current river banks, the river banks as they were in the 1700s, the outline of Fort Duquesne (the French presence), Fort Pitt (the English presence), and a turtle icon (found carved in a tree at that time) that represents the Native American presence. Carved into a black granite surround are the phrases, "Point of Confluence," "Point of Conflict," and "Point of Renewal," which are the three interpretive themes of Point State Park.

162 ART DIRECTORS CLUB ANNUAL IPAD CASE | Design Firm: RM&CO
Client: Art Directors Club of New York | Designer: Pete Rossi | Project Manager: Craig Dalton
Production Manager: Zack Kinslow | Production Company: DODOcase
Executive Director: Ignacio Oreamuno

Assignment: The Art Directors Club of New York commissioned us to design a limited edition iPad case to coincide with the first time in the ADC's 92-year history that no awards annual will be printed.

Approach: A custom-made DODOcase, to commemorate the launch of the ADC annual app. We worked with DODOcase to design a handcrafted iPad case inspired by the classic Art Directors Annuals from the 1920's. We wanted to create a timeless design coupled with that historic and handcrafted element. A classic yet contemporary case that celebrates and pays homage to the 92-year history of the ADC. The design features elements of the old, fused with the new. One of these classic elements is the medallion embossed on the back of the case, which was resurrected from a coin designed by sculptor Paul Manship in 1920 to honor the best creative work in the world. The launch of the 92nd Annual App is quite significant.

Results: It's the first time in the ADC's history that no book is printed, in the traditional sense. It's a big statement to the industry about how information can be consumed. In lieu of a printed book, the case acts as a tangible symbol for ADC members to hold in their hands. In honor of the ADC's fierce commitment to high-quality craftsmanship, this beautiful, intricate case was hand-made in San Francisco, California, using traditional techniques.

163, 164 HERBEAU | Design Firm: HI(NY) Design | Client: St.Louis International Inc., SSC Limited | Designers/ Art Directors: Hitomi Watanabe, Iku Oyamada | Website: www.hiny-design.com | Photographer: Akira Kawahata | Agency: HI(NY) Design

Assignment: HerBEAU is a new skincare line of phytotherapeutic products. It was created in 2013 by St. Louis International Inc. and SSC Limited in Japan. HI(NY)'s assignment was to create luxurious packaging for four products in this high-end herbal line, including a logo that represents the brand's personality: Natural, elegant, and decidedly feminine.

Approach: We conveyed the product's qualities through airy colors, delicate fonts and a clean layout. We used gradients for the product containers and diagonal graphics for the corresponding boxes, using the same color schemes. To give the packaging an even richer feel, we printed the logo on the outside, but then printed the gradient on the inside of the bottles. The result was a much richer look and feel. We also coated the paper of the box with a matte finish that felt sophisticated yet more natural than a typically glossy approach.

Results: Through careful management of the printing process, both on the boxes and inside the much more difficult-to-manage round containers, HI(NY) created packages that have a depth and elegance that match the luxury standards of the product. Sales of HerBEAU have been excellent and have confirmed our unique approach to this unique product. The final result was so well received that we have been asked to create three more product packages for HerBEAU.

165 CHRISTMAS BOX NO.15 | Design Firm: Stranger & Stranger
Client: Stranger & Stranger | Designers: Cosimo Surace, Guy Pratt, Francesco Graziani
Art Director: Kevin Shaw

Assignment: Create a special package to announce the launch of a spirits range.

Approach: Our aim was to get noticed with a range of cool, covetable brand shirts in special edition packaging.

166, 167 OSCAR MAYER BUTCHER THICK CUT BACON
Design Firm: Landor Associates | Client: Oscar Mayer | Designer: Strom Strandell
Production Artist: Ed Sarge | Naming/Writing Manager: Phyllis Murphy
Graphis Implementation Coordinator: J. Scott Hosa | Account Manager: Virginia Hultman
Executive Creative Director: Christopher Lehmann | Design Director: Anne Vaschetto
Account Management: Michael Bowman

Assignment: Butcher Thick Cut Bacon is Oscar Mayer's most premium product. Hearty, smoky, meaty goodness expertly cleaved into succulent slices, it's the stuff dreams are made of. But in reality, consumers weren't buying it—mainly because they couldn't see it. Lost in a sea of yellow, red and black, this king of cuts was anything but dominant at shelf. Even when consumers did stumble upon it, they couldn't tell what made Butcher Cut Bacon so special. To them, it just looked like more of the same with a higher price tag.

What Butcher Thick Cut needed was a big bold look to go along with its big bold flavor and premium price.

Approach: After a visual audit of the category, we noticed something interesting about bacon packaging. Most of the real estate isn't on the front of pack. It's on the back. Which happens to be the side that faces down at shelf. So we flipped our bacon over. Using the back panel as the front, we tripled the amount of space we had to work with—while instantly differentiating Butcher Thick Cut from every other bacon on the shelf. Then we turned up the heat and brought in the real, with an authentic, butcher-style paper substrate and precision-crafted type so traditional, it feels new all over again.

Results: So far, results have been epic, with sales increasing significantly since the new packaging hit shelves in August 2013. Moreover, our design is being used internally by Oscar Mayer as a means of inspiring and driving better design across their entire product portfolio. "Like nothing the category has ever seen…"—Julie Schaubroeck, Senior Marketing Director, Oscar Mayer

168 12 DAYS OF CHOCOLATE | Design Firm: Chase Design Group
Client: Chase Design Group | Designers: Jinny Bae, Jon Arriaza, David San Miguel, Paula Hansanugrum, Evangeline Joo, Beverly Hartono, Stephanie Kuga, Hea Kim
Director: Stephanie Goralnick | Creative Directors: Margo Chase, Clark Goolsby

Assignment: Every year Chase Design Group creates a holiday gift to share with clients. For 2013 we hit upon the idea of doing a chocolate gift. A humorous riff on the "12 Days of Christmas" seemed like the perfect way to feature Chase's inventive design and Clear Image's outstanding printing.

Approach: Each wrapper features a different aspect of the design process from frayed nerves to a perfect proof. Every designer at Chase got a chance to design their own wrapper both inside and out.

Results: Each design uniquely conveys the hectic and often humorous experience of working as a designer.

169 HP CHROMEBOOK 11 | Design Firm: Liquid Agency | Client: HP
Designers: Jeff Gardner, Google, Uneka | Project Coordinator: Janie Ramos
Production Company: Be Green Packaging | Creative Director: Diane Stember-Richards
Client Support: Priscilla Rodrigues

Assignment: The HP Chromebook is an ultra-minimalist and super affordable device designed to make it possible for more people to have access to the Internet. Along with our client, we agreed that the packaging solution should echo the qualities of the product, focusing on simplicity and minimalism. Specifically, we wanted to do less, not more.

Approach: The inspiration for the final package came from a humble take-out box that is perfectly functional while also being compostable. Liquid worked closely with the client's structural packaging designers and started an experimental design process that required both diligence and risk—and ultimately led to an innovative new packaging solution.

Results: The deceptively simple-looking box had to meet high standards for shipping at various temperatures and required multiple rounds of testing for structural integrity. The process even required making new machines that could create the box's unique shape and density. It was not easy to meet all the packaging requirements, but our client was committed to doing something extraordinary. And—by working as a team—we created a box that is minimalist not only in terms of aesthetics but also in terms of its environmental impact.

170 ORPHAN BARREL | Design Firm: Raison Pure NYC | Client: Diageo
Designer: Kyle Wessel | Production Manager: Miguel Altagracia
Partner/Creative Director: Laurent Hainaut | Illustrators: Grady McFerrin, Sam Gomez
Creative Director: JB Hartford | Account Manager: Rebecca Etter

Assignment: Raison Pure NYC collaborated with the North American Innovation team at Diageo to create Orphan Barrel. Orphan Barrel, a new to world brand, was created to find forgotten barrels of rare and delicious whiskey hidden away in rickhouses and distilleries. Tenets important to the brand are craft, quality and authenticity—each touchpoint from hand drawn labels to the bottling line reflect how these tenants are core beliefs lived by the brand.

Approach: The Orphan Barrel branding uses a rough-hewn hand drawn brandmark and a color palette of grays, browns and golds echoing the materials and colors from the rickhouses and distilleries where these barrels are found. The branding for Orphan Barrel remains consistent with each launch to announce all variants as members of the family, but the individual issues have their own personalities with animals that express the unique character of liquid and name. There are currently two brands launched: 20-year-old Barterhouse Whiskey and 26-year-aged Old Blowhard Whiskey. Both brands are expected to begin appearing on select shelves throughout the U.S. in March 2014 under strict allocation due to limited supply. Barterhouse Whiskey has a vintage khaki and brown label meant to look like a trade post circular featuring a sly fox as a salesman. Its substrate is a thick stock toothy paper meant to feel like a circular, and to communicate craft. Old Blowhard is a beautiful nautical blue label featuring a whale exhaling through its blowhole before launching into another opinionated debate. Powerful fonts rooted in swagger proclaim the spirit's impressive age statement and status as Kentucky Straight Bourbon. Each label was hand lettered and drawn featuring metallic varnishes and foil stamps, each detail reinforces authenticity and craftsmanship.

Results: The program has been met with excitement within Diageo, as well as with the Bourbon connoisseur community. There have been multiple launch events in key markets celebrating the new brand, its liquid and the crafted design. Additionally the design work, and overall brand, are going to be featured as a best in class example at multiple Diageo-wide meetings on design and strategy.

171 COCA-COLA SOCHI 2014 OLYMPIC WINTER GAMES PACKAGING
Design Firm: Turner Duckworth Design: London & San Francisco
Client: The Coca-Cola Company North America | Designers: Melissa Chavez, Brian Steele
Production Artist: Jeff Ensslen | Illustrator: Thomas Hennessy | Design Director: Brian Steele

Credits & Commentary

Creative Directors: David Turner, Bruce Duckworth, Sarah Moffat
Account Supervisor: Jessica Rogers
Assignment: The client challenged us to create promotional Coca-Cola packaging for the Sochi 2014 Olympic Winter Games to communicate the idea that Coke and the Olympics are "best enjoyed together."
Approach: We created packaging designs that communicated the partnership with the Olympic Games, but also were clearly Coca-Cola. We unified the Coca-Cola Dynamic Ribbon with winter athlete poses. Radiating line shapes echo the ribbon to create the athlete form and convey a sense of speed and motion.

172 COCA-COLA TET 2014 | Design Firm: Rice Creative | Client: Coca-Cola
Designers: Nguyen Huynh Tran Khanh, Hai Nguyen Phu, Truc Dinh Thi Thuy
Project Manager: Lan Mai Ngoc Que
Creative Directors: Chi-An De Leo, Joshua Breidenbach

173 HANSON VODKA | Design Firm: Stranger & Stranger | Client: Hanson Homemade Spirits
Designer: Cosimo Surace | Art Director: Kevin Shaw
Assignment: Create branding for a brand new, family run Sonoma vodka brand.
Approach: Try to own California vodka with the branding, allude to the high level of craft with the hand finishing and clearly code the flavors.
Results: Secured distribution and PR.

174 RUNNING WALKER IPA | Design Firm: Hawkeye Communications
Client: Braman Brewery | Designer/Art Director: Justin McCoy
Illustrator: Steven Noble | Creative Director: Terry McCoy
Assignment: Design a visual identity and package design for Braman Brewery's inaugural line of beer, Running Walker IPA. The beer was named after the Running Walker hound, an iconic Texas hunting dog that tracks and hunts predators. The dogs are bold and courageous, even in the face of mountain lions and bobcats. The goal was to produce a package design that honored the tradition and courage behind the dog that protected the Texas plains.
Approach: Hawkeye commissioned an illustration of the Running Walker in its iconic empowered stance in the antique engraving style. The stance was one the Running Walker would take when it sensed a predator was near. The dog's markings were based on an old photograph taken of the family dog, Joe Braman, a Running Walker. The illustration was paired with woodblock, hand drawn and script typography that was fitting for a subject so steeped in tradition.
Results: The package design for Running Walker IPA was very well received. Besides loving the fact that his old companion was immortalized on a beer, the traditional approach to the illustration choice and typography design really catered to the Texas roots of the Braman family.

175 STOKELJ WINE LABELS | Design Firm: Spela Draslar S.P.
Client: Stokelj wines | Designer: Spela Draslar
Assignment: The mission was to redesign the identity which would properly represent the traditionally produced wines of high quality.
Approach: The Stokelj family winery is based on the hills above Vipavska Wally where the custom of wine growing is family business and dates back to the Roman times. Unique location, history, symbiosis and the family's dedication to the high standards of wine production were keystone for the design process. Ancestor's timeless messages carved in stone were inspiration and the model.
Results: The result was/is client's identification with new identity. The imagination is the power of creation and the spirit of every civilization.

176 HUDNOTTS | Design Firm: Taxi Studio Ltd | Client: Kate Hudnott
Designers: Casey Blackmore, Marie Jones | Typographer: Rob Clarke
Illustrators: Sam Hadley, Steve Noble | Copywriter: Lindsay Camp
Chief Creative Directors: Ryan Wills, Spencer Buck | Account Director: Kate Kew
Assignment: Kate's pride, so well concealed in her daily life, pours unstoppably into her fine flavoured spirits. However, her existing branding did not live up to the quality of her premium tipples – so she asked us to put that right.
Approach: There are two sides to Kate's character – the 'darker' one only emerging in her drinks. So to tie the two together, we used the seven deadly sins to segment the range. Each sin relates to an aspect of the product, and cleverly aligns with Kate's unswerving passion for concocting liquid perfection.

177 MASTERSON'S WHEAT, RYE AND BARLEY | Design Firm: Studio 32 North
Client: 35 Maple Street Spirits | Designer: Sallie Reynolds Allen | Copywriter: Elliott Allen
Contributor: August Sebastiani
Assignment: The assignment was to expand the Masterson's brand beyond Masterson's Rye to include Masterson's Wheat and Barley.
Approach: Since the original Masterson's Rye label was a newspaper column, it made sense that the next two labels should be formatted similarly. Yet they also needed to be clearly distinct. Thus, the two-column Wheat label and the three-column, wrapped label for the Barley. To provide even more distinction and visual interest, the Wheat label is aligned with the silkscreen to complete the Masterson signature, while the Barley features a single paper label that wraps around the bottle.
Results: The design extension provides a consistent brand, as well as a level of distinction that's befitting of each whiskey.

178 BLAKE'S HARD CIDER LOGO/LABEL | Design Firm: McCann Detroit
Client: Blake's Cider Mill and Orchard | Designer: Adam Yarbrough

179 BOMBAY AMBER | Design Firm: Brand Union | Client: Bacardi | Designers: Glenn Tutssel, Olly Rudd | Production Manager: Andrew Smith | Creative Director: Glenn Tutssel
Account Director: Fiona Brady

180 JACK DANIEL'S SINATRA SELECT | Design Firm: Cue
Creative Director: Alan Colvin | Art Director: Sam Gardner
Client: Jack Daniel Distillery | Designers: Nathan Hinz, Alan Colvin
Assignment: Jack Daniel's Sinatra Select is a special edition whiskey crafted to honor Frank Sinatra's fifty-year friendship with Jack Daniel's. Frank was a fiercely loyal, lifetime fan of the brand, and Sinatra Select was designed to be both a classic expression of style and an homage to two American icons. This exclusive outpouring of the distiller's craft is matured in proprietary oak barrels for a bold flavor, timeless character and exceptional smoothness. Frank Sinatra lived a style that was truly his own. His independent spirit made him stand out in his time, and continues to distinguish him today. The design for Sinatra Select needed to balance Jack Daniel's legacy and Frank Sinatra's legacy with a look that is sleek and stylish, a reflection of Sinatra's timeless good taste.
Approach: The vessel designed for Jack Daniel's Sinatra Select is a taller, sleeker interpretation of the Jack Daniel's Tennessee Whiskey bottle, with a weighted base, an embossed metal shoulder label and a medallion featuring an icon of Frank's familiar fedora. Sinatra Select incorporates many of the brand's defining elements, and adds new ones specific to this expression. The capsule features the Jack Daniel's Country Club logo created by Frank to adorn a blazer he wore in the 1950s—a statement of his independent way of living. Sinatra Select is packaged within a bespoke bottle made for this special edition product. The branded box incorporates a medallion with the Frank Sinatra fedora icon and orange ribbon. The color orange works as the perfect complement to Sinatra Select's classic black color palette. Sinatra said that orange is the happiest color, and often used a bright orange pocket handkerchief to add some pop to his tailored suits and tuxedos. Inside is a special book that tells more about the story of Frank's fifty-year relationship with Jack Daniel's.
Results: A long-developing project partnership between Brown-Forman and the Frank Sinatra estate, Sinatra Select is now available at high-end retail stores and major airports worldwide. The product debuted in Las Vegas and has spread to destinations including New York, London, Sydney and Singapore. This super-premium offering from Jack Daniel's celebrates a man who lived without hesitation or compromise. Cue worked in collaboration with our partners at Brown-Forman Design from inception through sourcing, evaluating, and bringing the packaging to life. The result is a distinctive expression of style and grace, in keeping with the kindred spirit that it honors.

181 AMBER | Design Firm: Brand Union | Client: Pernod Ricard
Executive Director: Jonas Andersson | Design Director: Henrik Billqvist
Creative Directors: Mattias Lindstedt, Daniel Andersson | Designers: Wally Krantz, Taylor Simpson | Agency: Björn Atldax Vår/Woo

182 CALIFORNIA SQUARE WINE | Design Firm: Stranger & Stranger | Client: Truett Hurst
Designer: Cosimo Surace | Art Director: Kevin Shaw

183 UNDERLINE STUDIO HOLIDAY BEER PACKAGING | Design Firm: Underline Studio
Client: Underline Studio | Designer: Claire Dawson | Printer: Flash Reproductions
Creative Directors: Fidel Peña, Claire Dawson

184 FI MEETS THOMAS HUBER | Design Firm: beierarbeit | Client: Finanz Informatik
Photographer: Christian R. Schulz | Illustrator/Designer: Silke Nehring
Designer: Christoph Beier | Assistant: Patrick Witteck
Assignment: Thomas Huber is a famous German speed-climber who visited the Finanz Informatik on its Management-Congress in 2013 to speak about risk, adventure and success in the world of mountains. The aluminium travelling-bottles of SIGG were souvenirs for the visitors, possibly to get an autograph.

185 BALLAST POINT DEVIL'S SHARE WHISKEY | Design Firm: MiresBall
Client: Ballast Point Brewing & Spirits | Designer: Dylan Jones | Illustrator: Paul Elder
Photography Studio: Studioschulz.com | Creative Director: Scott Mires
Copywriter: David Fried | Account Director: Kristi Jones

186 MAC PRO PACKAGING | Design Firm: Apple
Client: Apple | Designer: Apple Marketing Communications
Approach: The packaging materials for Mac Pro were designed to emphasize the radical departure of the product from its previous form factor, and to reflect the powerful reengineered hardware. Provocative copy was employed to signal a new, confident attitude, as well as to challenge and inspire Mac Pro users.

187 TOBLERONE CHRISTMAS 2013 PACKAGING
Design Firm: Turner Duckworth: London & San Francisco | Client: Mondelez International
Designer: Butler Looney | Production Manager: James Norris | Illustrator: Martin Clarke
Design Director: Clem Halpin | Creative Directors: David Turner, Bruce Duckworth
Account Manager: Monica Annesanti

188 BLUE GOOSE | Design Firm: SID LEE | Client: Blue Goose
Designers: Anna Sera Garcia, Oleg Portnoy | Typographer: Ian Brignell
Production Companies: JIMMY LEE, M&H Graphics | Production Artist: Johnlee Raine
Print Producer: Karla Ramirez | Photographers: Rob Fiocca, Steve Krug
Illustrator: Ben Kwok | Executive Creative Director: Dave Roberts | Art Buyer: Emily Patterson
Creative Director: Tom Koukodimos | Copywriters: Pip Scowcroft, Laurent Abesdris, Ryan Spelliscy | Account Managers: Gabriel Sit, Matthew Bendavid
Account Director: Eve Remillard-Larose

189 DOMINO'S PAN PIZZA BOX | Design Firm: CP+B | Client: Domino's
Designer: Scott Pridgen | Traffic Manager: Alex Blumfelder | Studio: Brent Erb, Jeffrey Sloan, Cathy Dickinson | Print Producer: Duane Burgess | Photographer: Jessyel Ty Gonzalez
Illustrator: Roger Xavier | Executive Creative Director: Tony Calcao
Digital Artists: Zach Peutzer, Eduardo Santiesban | Design Director: Scott Pridgen
Creative Directors: Dave Steinke, Tom Miller | Copywriter: Sean Smith
Chief Creative Officer: Rob Reilly | Associate Creative Director: Mike Danko
Art Producer: Amy Foster | Account Supervisor: Tammie De Grasse-Cabrera, Alex Guerri, Meg Minkner | Account Manager: Michelle Robertson | Account Director: Evan Russack
Assignment: In 2012, CP+B was tasked with creating packaging for Domino's newest product, the Handmade Pan Pizza. The objective was to promote the new pizza nationwide, emphasizing the craft, care, time and pride put into Handmade Pan Pizza and distinguish it from other Domino's menu items. Domino's target audience is hard-working families who seek fast and convenient meals to fuel their busy lives. They look for value and quality in their food, which reinforced the importance of showcasing Domino's commitment to hand-made Pizza with fresh ingredients, right on the product's packaging.
Approach: To celebrate the launch of Domino's new Handmade Pan Pizza, we designed a special limited run of Pan Pizza boxes. The box design nods to the black pan the pizza is baked in, the craftsmanship of handset typography in

Credits&Commentary 245

Credits & Commentary

Victorian-era advertisements and the handcrafted Domino's Pan Pizza itself. The nearly all-black box is jam-packed with trivia, how-tos and fancy filigrees. Interesting facts found on the box include how the new recipe took three whole years to develop, and how each is made with fresh, never-frozen dough. Pizza boxes haven't been so elegantly informative until now.

Results: After weeks of concepting, we emerged with the boldest, sleekest packaging we've ever presented. Our clients were equally excited at the opportunity to release such an unexpected design to market and launched with a production run of 5,184,000 boxes across the US. We received an extremely positive consumer response to the box for both its unique design and its message that Domino's is rewriting the rules and launching a product that will make consumers rethink the quality of its pizza. The box received press recognition from The Denver Egotist, foodrepublic.com, GrubGrade, Packaging of the World, UnderConsideration and a slew of other various blogs. In the socialsphere, the box design garnered 1,628 total posts across Facebook, Twitter and Instagram—as well as 600,919 total potential impressions on Twitter alone.

190, 191 UPLAND TAP HANDLES | Design Firm: Young & Laramore
Client: Upland Brewing Company | Designer: Zac Neulieb | Writer: Scott King
Illustrator: Bruno Michaud | Executive Creative Director: Carolyn Hadlock
Creative Team: Taylor Schaffer | Creative Directors: Bryan Judkins, Trevor Williams
Account Manager: Nick Riedle | Account Director: Nick Prihoda

192 HELP PHILIPPINES | Design Firm: Jan Sabach Design
Client: Self initiated, American Red Cross | Designer: Jan Sabach

Assignment: Like most Designers, I felt helpless after the typhoon hit the Philippines. I can't get on a plane and help rebuild; my financial contribution is limited. Being in the visual communication business, I chose to use my skills to spread the word and motivate people to donate to the American Red Cross.

193, 194 SAGMEISTER SVA SUBWAY POSTERS
Design Firms: Sagmeister & Walsh, Visual Arts Press, Ltd. | Client: School of Visual Arts
Designers: Stefan Sagmeister, Jessica Walsh, Santiago Carrasquilla
Retoucher: Henry Leutwyler | Photographer: Erik Johansson
Design Director: Michael J. Walsh, Visual Arts Press, Ltd. | Art Directors: Stefan Sagmeister, Jessica Walsh | Executive Vice President, SVA: Anthony P. Rhodes

Assignment: SVA has a tradition of commissioning artists and designers to create posters that are displayed throughout New York City's Subway system.
Approach: The Fall 2013 SVA subway poster series were created by faculty members, Stefan Sagmeister (MFA Design) and Jessica Walsh (BFA Design), also, founders of design firm Sagmeister & Walsh. When SVA Executive Vice President, Anthony P. Rhodes, asked Sagmeister to create this season's design, the artist decided to focus on a universal theme: change. His attitude? Take It On.
Results: The octopus-topped man in one of the posters is Sagmeister himself. The second, featuring a woman's visage covered with graceful swoops of hair, like vines on a trellis, is Jessica Walsh. The final poster, of a man's face bursting with large block letters is SVA alumnus and Sagmeister & Walsh designer, Santiago Carrasquilla (BFA 2012 Graphic Design). The trio stare impassively ahead, their faces literally exuding the same message: Take It On.

195, 196 CITY OF SYDNEY BIKE POSTERS | Design Firm: Frost* Design
Client: City Of Sydney | Executive Creative Director: Vince Frost
Designer: Benjamin Hennessy | Creative Director: Anthony Donovan
Account Director: Brady Charlotte

Assignment: Frost* collaborated with the City of Sydney to create a graphic poster campaign featuring a bicycle-themed, hand-drawn font, to encourage bike riders to ride safely on the City's roads and new network of cycleways. Aimed at informing, educating and motivating bike riders to be aware of their riding behaviour on shared paths and roads, the City of Sydney briefed Frost* to set a new international standard for work designed to affect behavioural change.
Approach: The agency worked closely with the City of Sydney to develop a whimsical but arresting campaign that would cut through, generate conversation and motivate bikers to stop at red lights, slow down and take care on paths shared with pedestrians, as well as use the bell when passing. The creative team utilised the specialist skills of Frost* Design Director, Benjamin Hennessy, to develop a bespoke, hand-drawn type, which was then 3D rendered for an impactful realisation in print. Frost* tapped into the love of detail and appreciation of the hand-made, which is common amongst contemporary bicycle enthusiasts. The font was made of bike parts such as frames, handlebars, chains, seats, bells and brakes.

197 CINESCAPE | Design Firm: WONGDOODY | Client: Seattle International Film Festival
Designer: Ramon Vasquez | Retouching: Charlie Rakatansky
Project Manager: Barbara Wilson | Photography Studio: Juco Photo
Executive Creative Director: Tracy Wong | Electronic Production: Gail Savage, Kenta Hadley
Creative Director: Mark "Monkey" Watson | Copywriter: Peter Trueblood
Art Director: Adam Deer | Art Buyer: Jessica Obrist | Agency Producer: Molly Costin
Account Executive: Anea Klix | Account Director: Garth Knutson

Assignment: Annually since 1975, in mid-May the Seattle International Film Festival has taken over Seattle theaters for three entire weeks showing over 400 films. But to attract the non-festival-goer, it has to overcome the notion that film festivals are an intimidating affair, meant only for the hoity-toity film crowd. SIFF's breadth of offering can also be daunting, so we seek draw people in, encouraging them to take a peek and dive deeper.
Approach: SIFF films are an escape from reality, from our daily lives. They whisk us to faraway lands and introduce us to far-out ideas that we could never dream of. We can forget about our troubles, expand our minds and transport ourselves into another world, becoming another person. IT'S LIKE TAKING A VACATION FROM YOURSELF. So let's push that thought. Imagine that SIFF is a service that literally transports you to another world. It offers what we're calling a "Cinescape." Plucking you from your life and allowing you to become another person or live in another dimension — but only for a few hours. Then you're returned to your life the same... but different.

198 3D TYPE EXHIBITION | Design Firm: Dankook University | Designer: Hoon-Dong Chung
Assignment: This poster is designed for an experimental project 'Unstable Unity'. The project focuses on expanding 2D types into 3D environment.
Approach: Converting 2D types into 3D imagery / Expanding visualization possibilities in Typography

199 THEATRICAL POSTERS | Design Firm: peter bankov
Client: Teatr-Teatr theatrical center in Perm | Designer: Peter Bankov
Assignment: Create posters for the 2013 theatrical program in Perm, Russia.
Approach: Create actual modern posters for a theatrical season in Perm, Russia.

200 DAAP POSTER SERIES | Design Firm: Landor Associates
Client: University of Cincinnati (School of Design, Art, Architecture and Planning)
Designers: Akshata Wadekar, Tara Hush, Heather Ingram | Senior Designer: Tika Redding
Production Artist: Toni Doty | Executive Creative Director: Valerie Aurilio
Digital Artist/Multimedia: Sean Hafer | Design Director: Jay Hoffman

Assignment: One of the top design school in the nation, University of Cincinnati's School of Design, Art, Architecture and Planning asks alumni from today's leading design companies to create a poster for its annual senior showcase, DAAPWORKS.
Approach: The poster series elevates the DAAP identity as an empty vessel, ready to take on an infinite array of visuals that represent the eclectic experience of each student's journey as they begin making their mark on the professional world.
Results: Faculty and students embraced the poster series and used it to create a stunning showcase for their graduating class. "For the time I have been at DAAP, this concept is the best one—most definitely." – Professor Oscar Fernandez, UC

201 EPIC EYE POSTER 2 | Design Firm: IF Studio | Client: Epic Litho
Designers: Toshiaki Ide, Hisa Ide | Project Manager: Athena Azevedo
Photographer Studio: Henry Leutwyler Studio | Photographer: Henry Leutwyler
Creative Director: Toshiaki Ide | Design Director: Hisa Ide

Assignment: To create a poster to announce the upcoming release of "Epic Eye" magazine - an artistic collaboration between Epic Litho and IF STUDIO to showcase and celebrate the work of one accomplished visual artist. Issue no.1 features the work of photographer Henry Leutwyler.
Approach: To create emotional connection through images and design.

202 EPIC EYE POSTER | Design Firm: IF Studio | Client: Epic Litho
Designers: Toshiaki Ide, Hisa Ide | Project Manager: Athena Azevedo
Photography Studio: Henry Leutwyler Studio | Photographer: Henry Leutwyler
Creative Director: Toshiaki Ide | Design Director: Hisa Ide

Assignment: To create a poster to announce the upcoming release of "Epic Eye" magazine - an artistic collaboration between Epic Litho and IF STUDIO to showcase and celebrate the work of one accomplished visual artist. Issue no.1 features the work of photographer Henry Leutwyler.
Approach: To create emotional connection through images and design.

203, 204 STATE LEGISLATURES MAGAZINE POSTERS | Design Firm: 601 Design, Inc.
Client: National Conference of State Legislatures | Designer/Illustrator: Bruce Holdeman
Editor-in-Chief: Karen Hansen | Editor: Julie Lays

Assignment: Promotional posters for the upcoming issue State Legislatures magazine using that issue's cover illustration.
Approach: Most of the work on the art and headline had been worked out in the cover design phase of the magazine schedule. The posters are similarly formatted for fast production and are displayed as the magazine is sent for printing.

205 BRAZILIAN OPERA POSTER | Design Firm: IF Studio
Client: International Brazilian Opera Company | Designer: Toshiaki Ide, Hisa Ide
Design Director: Hisa Ide | Creative Director: Toshiaki Ide | Photographer: Athena Azevedo
Assignment: Conceptualize and design posters to announce the inaugural performances of the International Brazilian Opera Company in New York City.
Approach: Brand the Brazilian opera as a performance that is passionate, dramatic and modern high art.

206 KUBRICK POSTER | Design Firm: Landor Associates | Client: Stanley Kubrick Archive
Designer: Peter Knapp | Associate Creative Director: Ben Marshall

Assignment: A select group was chosen to attend a Private View of the Stanley Kubrick Archive. We created awareness, in a manner suiting the man and his work.
Approach: Inspired by both the Space Station and Obelisk in '2001: A Space Odyssey' we created an ominous Stanley Knife. Like the work of the man himself, our poster did not give itself away at first-viewing. It was supported by an invite and Stanley Knife blades etched with his signature and the event date.
Results: Full attendance, but with a lot of suitable intrigue prior to the event. The poster is now part of the archive at the request of the curator.

207 REFA CARAT | Design Firm: omdr Co.,Ltd. | Client: MTG Co.,Ltd.
Designer: Osamu Misawa

Assignment: MTG Co., Ltd is a company which develops innovative beauty treatment devices. This ReFa CARAT is a mega-hit product which has sold over 2 million units, allowing the company's name to gain a wider publicity. Having past five years since its release, we were tasked to cîreate a new main image which would enhance the brand's status as a part of re-branding attempt.
Approach: To achieve this goal, we used lightings which emphasize the jewel-like beauty of rollers against the backdrop of perfume bottles filled with water to produce an elegant image with full of light. While the overall base tone is in amber, small patches of red, blue, and green sown on it emphasize the stereoscopic effect and brilliance. The message underlying this image is our wish for women to shine bright with the help of 'micro-current' (very gentle electric current) which is used for this product.
Results: Initially, this design was intended for the use at limited locations (COLTON), but having received many favorable remarks, it was adopted for leaflets, store fixtures, and campaign posters (transportation advertising) used in shops nationwide. It is highly evaluated as an innovative, high-quality visual which totally recasts the branding in the past 5 years.

Credits & Commentary

208 UTSOA SPRING LECTURE SERIES POSTER | Design Firm: Dyal and Partners
Client: The University of Texas School of Architecture | Designer: Herman Dyal

209 THE ARTISTS HAVE CHECKED IN | Design Firm: Zulu Alpha Kilo
Client: Gladstone Hotel, Leila Courey | Designers: Ari Elkouby, Grant Cleland
Writer: George Ault | Production Artists: Jamie Morren, Brandon Dyson
Photographer: Arash Moallemi | Creative Director: Zak Mroueh
Agency Producers: Kate Spencer, Kari Macknight Dearborn
Account Supervisor: Vidas Kubilius | Account Directors: Niki Bartl, Nevena Djordjevic

210, 211 THE SYRO IPAD TOTE | Company: Sydney Rogers (Co- Founders Sydney Rogers, John Fiorentino) | Designer: Sydney Rogers | Photographer: Todd Martin
Co-Founders of Sydney Rogers, LLC.: Sydney Rogers, John Fiorentino.
Assignment: The goal was to create and design a product that integrated technology into fashion in a truly beautiful and awe-inspiring way. The technology needed to stay true to the artistry of the fashion aesthetic while still taking full advantage of the infinite possibilities of the digital world. Fashion has struggled with the adoption of technology and Sydney set out to solve that problem.
Approach: The challenge was to figure out how to harness both the beauty and power of technology with out diluting the classic fashion aesthetic and experience. After countless hours of design, both on the physical product and within the app, the SYRO tote was the perfect combination of fashion and technology.
Results: The result is the SYRO iPad Tote. Carrying the bag gives you a feeling like you've never felt before. There is a deeper connection with the SYRO Tote as you can interact with it and make it your own. It is truly a powerful and captivating product that delivers an unparalleled experience. The reactions and response to the infamous SYRO Tote have been incredible.

212 NONOBJECT SOAP | Design Firm: NONOBJECT | Client: NONOBJECT
Designer and Creative Director: Suncica Lukic | Junior Designer: Helene Bourdon (intern)
Copywriter: Malin Leschly

213 OPUS INTERNATIONAL CONSULTANTS | Design Firm: DNA
Client: Lauren Gibson, Mike Eagle | Designers: Phil Dunstan-Brown, Anna-Marie Antipas
Photographer: Ian Robertson | Account Director: Gill Coltart

214 RECYCLED BEAUTY | Client: Laurie Frankel Photography
Designers: Laurie Frankel, Diane Gatterdam | Producer: Aly Su Borst
Assignment: Create promotional mailers displaying images from the Recycled Beauty photo series. This collection paired and contrasted two kinds of decay, those of ordinary, unused trash items and of decomposing nature. The piece was sent to a select group of creatives.
Approach: We wanted to incorporate a light, delicate, and raw quality to the printing and packaging. The packaging fell apart as it was opened, almost breaking away and disintegrating. We used burned parchment paper which was crispy brown to wrap the piece. The images were printed on tissue paper and wrapped between chipboard which, in turn, was wrapped shut with vintage rough thread. A personal note to each recipient was included.
Results: Recycled Beauty received attention in both international and national trade press. We received many positive calls and emails from potential clients who expressed appreciation for both the imagery and the creativity of the packaging.

215 ALPHACHROME CARDS | Design Firm: Studio Hinrichs | Client: Studio Hinrichs
Designers: Kit Hinrichs, Dang Nguyen | Printer: Blanchette Press
Copywriter: Delphine Hirasuna
Assignment: Following the creation of Obsessions: The Alphabet Card, Kit Hinrichs was inspired by his collection of Victorian Alphabet Postcards to bring the tradition into the 21st Century.
Approach: The AlphaChrome Cards are a modern interpretation of original alphabet cards from the late 19th and early 20th centuries. The typeface used is an in-house revival of Stack, which was Dan X. Solo's 1970s typeface. The cards are made from 30 different prints, including William Morris patterns, Italian Marble Papers, and traditional Japanese Prints. The set consists of 39 cards: the full alphabet, 0 through 9, !, &, and ?.

216 IF STUDIO PROMOTIONAL POSTCARDS | Design Firm: IF Studio
Client: IF Studio | Designers: Toshiaki Ide, Hisa Ide | Design Director: Hisa Ide
Creative Director: Toshiaki Ide | Photographers: Tatijana Shoan, Michael Imlay, Jacob Snavely
Illustrators: Tara Hardy, Bil Donovan
Assignment: We wanted to announce Toshiaki and Hisa Ide's recent accomplishment as Graphis Design Masters to our clients and partners.
Approach: We printed promotional postcards with our award winning images and mailed the collection of 14 pieces to clients and partners.
Results: We loved the cards so much that we doubled the assignment. The spread of cards was photographed and used for the IF Studio email signature.

217 BREAKAWAY JERSEY | Design Firm: Weymouth Design | Client: CYCLE Kids
Designer: Chip Griffin | Creative Director: Robert Krivicich
Assignment: The jerseys for the Breakaway event needed to appeal to the wide range of people who would ride in the event but most importantly to cyclists who would wear the jersey, further promoting the Breakaway event.
Approach: As ride leaders would be at the front of the group, the back of their jerseys had bold stripes and a different color shield so they were easily identified.

218 LETTERPRESS CURRENCY REDESIGN PROJECT | Design Firm: BRED
Client: BRED (self-initiated) | Designer: Ned Drew
Assignment: This self-initiated project was inspired in part by W. A. Dwiggins' 1932 proposal Towards a Reform of the Paper Currency. This experimental investigation was also created to showcase and promote a new type family recently designed by our studio – Ludd.
Approach: I wanted to try and retain the spirit of the current US bills while contrasting the more iconic elements with a humorous look at American history and its myths. Formally I was reacting to the conservative nature and blandness of our bills, trying to develop a more dynamic composition and impression without losing the narratives. This three-part, letterpress currency series ($5, $10 and

$20) was an exploration into color – how to use color to develop a dynamic single composition while developing a system and family of bills. The production included several passes through the press and these bills are built of 6 to 8 different spot colors, some florescent and some specially mixed.
Results: Being both designer and client provided me with several distinctive advantages. While representing the dynamic quality of the typeface through the letterpress process I was also able to use an older technology with contemporary software towards a unique application and result. I wanted the halftones to have perfect registration and details, the layers to be dense and complex, all with zero impression. When first looking at these prints most people believe they are inkjet prints! These prints acted as both a teaser for the type family and as a visual representative of the idiosyncratic nature of this quirky typographic system and its complexities.

219 KING OF DENMARK | Design Firm: Concrete Design Communications | Client: Cava
Designer: Ty Whittington | Creative Directors: Diti Katona, John Pylypczak

220 NONOBJECT PASTA | Design Firm: NONOBJECT | Client: NONOBJECT
Designer and Creative Director: Suncica Lukic | Junior Designer: Helene Bourdon (intern)
Copywriter: Malin Leschly

221, 222 GOETTA JOB! (RECRUITING FRESH MEAT) | Design Firm: Interbrand
Client: Interbrand | Designer: Jenny Pohlman | Senior Designers: Jenn Talbot,
Scott Cunningham | Production Manager: Jack Hinkel | Photographer: Jeff Tilford
Executive Creative Director: Jamey Wagner | Digital Artist: Ken Kirby
Art Director: Shane Jallick | Account Manager: Will Kladakis

223 WEBSTER RETRI AERO Design Firm: Webster | Client: Webster | Designer: Nate Perry
Writer: Jason Fox | Printer: Porridge Paper | Creative Director: Dave Webster
Assignment: Every year Webster designs a limited edition fun creative gift for our clients and colleagues. This year we created Webster Retro Aero:
Some – citing dictionaries, Latin roots and commonly accepted definitions – would say a trilogy consists of tree parts. To that we say, "Fie!" Partly because we love old-timey, pseudo-Irish slang, and partly because this bit of work is obviously Part IV in our Tin Toy Trilogy. Obviously. Once again of a limited edition and sought after by discerning, if socially awkward, collectors worldwide. But, for the first time, featuring letterpress printing.
Approach: We started with the tin toy, a retro aero plane and proceeded to wrap it in awesome. With graphics calling back to the days of air mail and a shiny tin to encase the also shiny tin toy, our annual holiday mailing again met our goal of "fun." We increased the touchability factor by letterpressing all of the printed art.
Results: We are our own clients on this and we couldn't be happier with the results. We also received a massive amount of positive replies from our actual clients, who received these little wonders in the mail. In addition, the Retro Aero also landed on many design blogs throughout the industry.

224, 225 BOISSONS DE MADAME BABINEAUX | Design Firm: Ultra Creative
Client: Ultra Creative Client Gift | Designers: Jessica Ward Hill, JoEllen Martinson Davis,
William Burns, Jen Sheeler | Production: Todd Schneider
Printer: First Impressions Group | Copywriter: Megan Auld-Wright

226, 227 LITTLE BRITCHES RODEO - PROMOTION PIECE | Design Firm: HY Connect
Client: John Sibilski Photography | Designer: Jeff Jasinowski
Production Managers: Robin Finco, Carol Rockow
Executive Creative Director: Mark Catterson

228, 229 PROPOSITION CHICKEN RESTAURANT BRANDING
Design Firm: Rebecca Bartlett LLC | Client: Wednesday Seven
Designer/Copywriter: Rebecca Bartlett
Assignment: It's all about choice. Or, at least it should be when it comes to eating chicken in San Francisco. When Wednesday Seven came to us with their latest foodie concept — a restaurant that serves nothing but chicken — we were tasked with naming it, branding it and making it the catchiest counter concept in town.
Approach: You could say we went full chicken. We started with brand strategy, naming and positioning, then took the bird from concept to counter by designing the logo, menus, brand collateral, packaging, exterior/interior decor, and signage.
Results: Proposition Chicken was an instant success among customers and the press. The concept and brazen branding received acclaim in Urban Daddy, Thrillist, Eater, and Inside Scoop SF.

230, 231 SMALL BATCH | Design Firm: TOKY | Client: Baileys' Restaurants
Designer: Travis Brown | Executive Creative Director: Eric Thoelke

232, 233 JONES BROS. CUPCAKES – WEST | Design Firm: Webster
Client: Jones Bros. Cupcakes | Designer: Loucinda Heinert
Illustrator: Sean Heisler | Creative Director: Dave Webster
Assignment: Jones Bros. Cupcakes is a local, family-owned bakery and cafe, specializing in gourmet cupcakes. After booming success at their first location, Jones Bros. came to us again to help with the branding of their new West Omaha location. We worked closely with the architects and contractors to bring the flavor of the Jones Bros. brand to life both inside and outside the building.

234 ADOPT-A-PET STAMPS | Design Firm: Subplot Design Inc. | Client: Canada Post
Designer: Ross Chandler | Production Designers: Matthew Clark, Liz Wurzinger
Photography Studio: Raina + Wilson | Photographer: Raeff Miles
Illustrators: Monika Melnychuk, Steph Gibson
Creative Directors: Matthew Clark, Roy White

235 DEATH TO DEATH | Design Firm: Sumo | Client: National Galleries Scotland
Designer: Gavin Downey

236 KRIMTH INC. | Design Firm: KEI TAKIMOTO | Client: Krimth Inc.
Designer/Art Director: Kei Takimoto

Index

DESIGN FIRMS

160over90 24, 25
21xdesign 32, 33
601 Design, Inc. 203, 204
9 Threads 115, 116
Addison 22, 23
AG Creative 157
Alt Group 155
Apple 186
Arcana Academy 64
AS IF Media Group, LLC. 107-109
Ayşe Çelem Design 82
Bailey Lauerman 156
BEAMY 83
beierarbeit 184
Brand Union 179, 181
BRED 218
Chase Design Group 160, 168
Concrete Design Communications 129, 219
Connelly Partners / ISMCP 77
CP+B 189
Craig-Teerlink Design 157
Cue 180
DAE 78, 81
Dankook University 198
Design is Play 155, 157
Dessein 88
DNA 213
Dyal and Partners 208
Faith 104-106
Fellow 41, 148
Flake 159
Founded by Design 65
Frost* Design 195, 196
GQ 92-99
Graham Hanson Design 152
Hawkeye Communications 157, 174
Headcase Design 28, 29
HI(NY) Design 163, 164
HOOK 158
Hoyne 70, 71
H.Tuncay Design 159
HUSH Studios 145
HY Connect 226, 227
IDEAS360° | SG360° a Segerdahl company 139, 140
IF Studio 68, 69, 201, 202, 205, 216
INNOCEAN USA 141, 143
Intellecta Corporate 20, 21
Interbrand 56, 57, 221, 222
Jan Sabach Design 192
KEI TAKIMOTO 236
KMD Inc. 120, 121, 128
Landesberg Design 161
Landor Associates 67, 166, 167, 200, 206
Laurie Frankel Photography 214
Leap 160
Leynivopnid 157
lg2boutique 42, 43, 46, 47, 50, 51, 66
Lippincott 38, 39, 44, 45, 48, 49, 134, 135
Liquid Agency 155, 169
Lorenc+Yoo Design Inc 126, 127
Mason Zimbler 144
McCann Detroit 178
Mermaid, Inc. 155
Michael Schwab Studio 150, 159
MiresBall 185
mkcreative 160
Monogram 149
Morla Design 58, 59
NONOBJECT 212, 220
Nuno Duarte Martins 27
Odear 155
omdr Co.,Ltd. 207
Parallax Design 122, 123
Pentagram 36, 37, 100-103, 114, 160
Peppermill Projects 150
peter bankov 199
Peter Schmidt Group 110
Piera Wolf 112, 113
Poulin+Morris Inc. 118, 119, 124, 125, 132, 133
Publicis Kaplan Thaler 60, 61
Raison Pure NYC 170
Ralph Appelbaum Associates 136, 137
Rebecca Bartlett LLC 228, 229
Regina Rubino / Robert Louey 130, 131
Rice Creative 26, 172
Risd Class of 2013 138
RM&CO 162
Sagmeister & Walsh 193, 194
Shadia Design 62, 63
Shamlian Creative 154
SID LEE 188
SMOG Design, Inc. 30, 31
Spela Draslar S.P. 175
Squires & Company 156
Steven Taylor Associates 76
Stranger & Stranger 165, 173, 182
Studio 32 North 177
Studio Hinrichs 84, 86, 87, 215
Subplot Design Inc. 234
Sumo 235
Sydney Rogers, LLC 210, 211
Taxi Studio Ltd 176
The Designory 72, 73
The General Design Co. 155, 159
The Office of Gilbert Li 54, 55
The Partners 151
The Rivalry 152, 153
The White Room Inc 117, 146
Timberland In-House 85
TOKY 230, 231
Toolbox Design 74, 75, 158
Toppan Printing Co., Ltd. 79, 80
Turner Duckworth Design: London & San Francisco 171, 187
Ultra Creative 224, 225
Underline Studio 111, 183
University of Wisconsin-Green Bay 142
Visual Arts Press, Ltd. 89, 193, 194
Wallace Church, Inc 147
Webster 223, 232, 233
Weymouth Design 217
White Studio 34, 35
WONGDOODY 197
WPA Pinfold 40, 52, 53, 90, 91
xose teiga, studio. 160
Young & Laramore 190, 191
Zulu Alpha Kilo 209

DESIGNERS

Abbot, Rodney 48, 49, 134, 135
Allen, Sallie Reynolds 177
Amador, Jorge 34, 35
Amborn, Jesse 155
Ancalmo, Carlos 145
Antipas, Anna-Marie 213
Apple Marketing Communications 186
Ardzivian, Ani 118, 119
Arriaza, Jon 168
Atkin, Trudi 52, 53
Arzoo, Derek 143
Ayling, Sam 38, 39, 44, 45
Bae, Jinny 168
Bailey, Ryan 156
Balbarin, John 68, 69
Bankov, Peter 199
Banton, Brian 54, 55
Bartlett, Rebecca 228, 229
Beier, Christoph 184
Blackmore, Casey 176
Boske, Karl-Magnus 155
Bours, Benjamin 93, 94, 97
Braceros, Nathan 108, 109
Brickell, Caroline 159
Brickell, Carrie 155
Brown, Travis 230, 231
Burns, William 224, 225
Campbell, Nancy 115, 116
Cardinal, Chelsea 92, 95, 96, 98
Carrasquilla, Santiago 193, 194
Carrillo, Andreina 124, 125, 132, 133
Cech, Jay 155
Çelem, Ayşe 82
Chandler, Ross 234
Chavez, Melissa 171
Chung, Hoon-Dong 198
Chung, Woo 67
Church, Stan 147
Chiu, Andrew 48, 49, 134, 135
Cleland, Grant 209
Colvin, Alan 180
Coonrod, Matt 72, 73
Côté, Serge 46, 47, 50, 51
Craig-Teerlink, Jean 157
Crouchman, Ryan 129
Dawson, Claire 111, 183
Deetz, Kristy 142
Delgado, Carla 100-103
Dinh Thi Thuy, Truc 172
Downey, Gavin 235
Draslar, Spela 175
Drew, Ned 218
Duarte Martins, Nuno 27
Dugas, Matt 77
Dunstan-Brown, Phil 213
Dyal, Herman 208
Eagleton, Nick 151
Elkouby, Ari 209
Engqvist, Kornelia 26
Esseveld, Alex 64
Fox, Mark 155, 157
Frankel, Laurie 214
Fry, Barrett 36, 37, 114, 160
Gardner, Jeff 169
Gatterdam, Diane 214
Geroni, Ralph 28, 29
Glover, Patrick 90, 91
Google 169
Gray, Ben 145
Graziani, Francesco 165
Griffin, Chip 217
Gunderson, Will 41, 148
Gylfason, Einar 157
Haire, Lauren 149
Hansanugrum, Paula 168
Hanson, Graham 152
Hartono, Beverly 168
Heikkinen, Eero 159
Heinert, Loucinda 232, 233
Hennessy, Benjamin 195, 196
Herter, Erik 118, 119, 132, 133
Hiek, Gloria 84
Hinkelbein, Gerrit 110
Hinrichs, Kit 84, 86, 87, 215
Hinz, Nathan 180
Hogan, Christina 145
Hohmann, Marc 38, 39, 44, 45
Holdeman, Bruce 203, 204
Hosokawa, Natsuko 128
Hoyne, Andrew 70, 71
Hush, Tara 200
Huynh Tran Khanh, Nguyen 172
Ide, Hisa 68, 69, 201, 202, 205, 216
Ide, Toshiaki 68, 69, 201, 202, 205, 216
Ilich, Stjepan 67
Ingram, Heather 200
Irizarry, Daniel 107
Jallick, Shane 56, 57
Jariya, Jade 58, 59
Jasinowski, Jeff 226, 227
Jointe, Andre 93, 96, 99
Jones, Dylan 185
Jones, Marie 176
Joo, Evangeline 160, 168
Jung, Stewart 157
Kaczmarek, Jesse 152, 153
Kang, Michelle 160
Kepple, Paul 28, 29
Kim, Hea 168
Knapp, Peter 206
Krantz, Wally 181
Krstic, Goran 145
Kwon, Jung 48, 49, 134, 135
Kuga, Stephanie 168
Lam, Gigi 78
Landesberg, Rick 161
Laube, Bart 56, 57
Larsen, Imri 38, 39, 44, 45
Lee, Esther 88
Lee, Ronn 83
Lescarbeau, Maude 66
Liu, Mac 126, 127
Loboda, Karolina 146
Looney, Butler 187
Lorenc, Jan 126, 127
Louie, Bryan 145
Louie, Wes 145
Lukic, Suncica 212, 220
Mac Cormack, Dermot 32, 33
Madison, Kipp 161
Maegawa, Junko 67
Marois, Marilyn 42, 43
Martinson Davis, JoEllen 224, 225
McCandliss, Trevett 115, 116
McCoy, Justin 174
McLaughlin, Sharon 155
McMahon, Chris 40, 90, 91
Michael Schwab Studio Elixir Design 159
Miles, Bryan 144
Miller, Chad 24, 25

Index

Misawa, Osamu......207
Miyazaki, Kei......120, 121, 128
Monahan, Jeff......160
Mondes de Oca, Leonor......48, 49, 134, 135
Morcos, Wael......138
Morla, Jennifer......58, 59
Mui, Kai......81
Muñoz, John......93
Najera, Ivan......144
Nehring, Silke......184
Neulieb, Zac......190, 191
Nguyen, Dang......86, 87, 215
Nguyen Phu, Hai......172
Ogawa, Masahiro......79, 80
Ohanessian, Shadia......62, 63
Oltman, Brandon......156
Oyamada, Iku......163, 164
Palmbäck, Thomas......155
Pantuso, Michael......139, 140
Peña, Fidel......111
Perry, Nate......223
Peterson, Hannah......150
Petrina, Joe......161
Phillips, Joshua......154
Pinfold, Myles......40

Pinilla, Diego......108
Podlogar, Chelsea......22
Pohlman, Jenny......221, 222
Poole, Dean......155
Portnoy, Oleg......188
Pratt, Guy......165
Presiado, Arnie......141
Pridgen, Scott......189
Purtilar, Chet......48, 49, 134, 135
Ralph Appelbaum Associates......136, 137
Ramos, Alfonso......157
Rei, Raquel......34, 35
Remphrey, Matthew......122, 123
Rodman, Neil......124, 125
Rogers, Sydney......210, 211
Rossi, Pete......164
Rouette, Andrée......42, 43, 46, 47
Rubino, Regina......130, 131
Rudd, Olly......179
Rutherford, Emma......40
Sabach, Jan......192
Sagmeister, Stefan......193, 194
Salyer, Andre......145
San Miguel, David......168
Schmidt, Anders......20, 21

Schwab, Michael......150
Scott, Aaron......160
Sera Garcia, Anna......188
Sheeler, Jen......224, 225
Sim, Kay......24, 25
Simões, Ana......34, 35
Simpson, Taylor......181
Smart, Andrew......122, 123
Stark, Veronica......74, 75, 158
Steele, Brian......171
Steinhardt, Nick......30, 31
Strandell, Strom......166, 167
Surace, Cosimo......165, 173, 182
Sych, Paul......104-106
Takimoto, Kei......236
Taylor, Steven......76
Teiga, Xose......160
The, Cassia......67
Thrasher, Christy......130, 131
Tobin, E. Patrick......89
Tomita, Hideaki......120, 121
Thomas, Chris......65
Tuncay, Haluk......159
Tutssel, Glenn......179
Uneka......169

Valdis, Unnur......157
Vasquez, Ramon......197
Vollmöller, Bernd......110
Wadekar, Akshata......200
Waggoner, Brady......158
Wainwright, Karen......154
Wall, Hayley......40
Walsh, Jessica......193, 194
Walters, Lee......64
Wang, Angie......155, 157
Ward Hill, Jessica......224, 225
Watanabe, Hitomi......163, 164
Wessel, Kyle......170
Whittington, Ty......219
Winkler, Marissa......67
Wolf, Piera......112, 113
Wood, Greg......77
Wyllie, Lauren......70, 71
Yang, Erik......145
Yarbrough, Adam......178
Yeaton, Tom......85
Yoo, Chung......126, 127
Yuen, Kin......23
Yule, Jonathon......129

CLIENTS

35 Maple Street Spirits......177
"A Trip to the Moon" Film and Production Company......159
Allegheny Trail Alliance......161
American Red Cross......192
Angels & Cowboys......150
Ango Mode......50, 51
Anthony Gismondi......158
Apple......186
Arcana Academy......64
Art Directors Club of New York......162
Art Gallery of Mississauga......117
AS IF Magazine......107-109
Bacardi......179
Bad Robot......28, 29
Baileys' Restaurants......230, 231
Ballast Point Brewing & Spirits......185
BLACK+DECKER......38, 39
Black Swan State Theatre Company......88
Blake's Cider Mill and Orchard......178
Braman Brewery......174
BRED......218
BRIC......124, 125
Caffe Aficionado......159
Câmara Municipal de Guimarães – Arquivo Municipal Alfredo Pimenta......34, 35
Canada Post......234
Cava......219
Cenveo......23
Chase Design Group......168
Citibank......60, 61
City Of Sydney......195, 196
Clinic Blanco Ramos......160
Coca-Cola......172
Coca-Cola Turkey......82
Council for Hakka Affairs......128
Croots......52, 53
CYCLE Kids......217
Danielli's Fine Foods......65
Department of Further Education, Employment, Science and Technology......122, 123
DHA Capital and Continental Properties, Cantor & Pecorella, Inc.......68, 69
Diageo......170

digital arts......155
Dinosaur Designs......70, 71
Domino's......189
Earnshaw's magazine......116
Eaton......136, 137
Epic Litho......201, 202
Erin Tracy......146
Event Academy......159
Ficks......155
Film and Video Umbrella......151
Finanz Informatik......184
First & First Creative Real Estate......41, 148
Flash Reproductions Ltd.......111
Footwear Plus magazine......115
fshnunlimited magazine......104-106
Gladstone Hotel......209
Google......152, 153
Google New York......152
GQ......92-99
Granum A/I......132, 133
Hanson Homemade Spirits......173
Heesen......76
Hillerich & Bradsby Co.......56, 57
History Will Be Kind......149
HP......169
Hyatt Regency, New Orleans, LA.......126, 127
Hyundai Motor America......141, 143
IF Studio......216
Images Festival......54, 55
Infiniti Motors Ltd.......72, 73
Intellecta......20, 21
Interbrand......221, 222
International Brazilian Opera Company......205
iStar Financial......22
Jack Daniel Distillery......180
Johanne Demers (founder of La Vittoria)......42, 43
John Sibilski Photography......226, 227
Jones Bros. Cupcakes......232, 233
Kate Hudnott......176
Kenny Braun/University of Texas Press......36, 37
Kestrel Aircraft......160
Kirkstall Brewery......40
Koganei-shi, City Office......120, 121
Komori Corporation......79, 80

Krimth Inc.......236
Landor Associates......67
Lauren Gibson and Mike Eagle......213
Laurie Frankel Photography......214
Leila Courey......209
Lisa S. Johnson......30, 31
Los Angeles Boulders......155
Loyola Marymount University......114
MapR Technologies......157
Mark and Joumana Norris......62, 63
Marty Grims......154
Mason Zimbler......144
Melcher Media......28, 29
Mondelez International......187
Monotype......48, 49, 134, 135
MTG Co.,Ltd.......207
Mulholland Books......28, 29
National Conference of State Legislatures......203, 204
National Galleries Scotland......235
National Grid......90, 91
Nebraska Antique Farming Association......156
Nerdin St. Rose......77
New Zealand Opera......155
NONOBJECT......212, 220
NPR......118, 119
Odear Open......155
Old Ox Brewery......150
Oscar Mayer......167, 168
Palmieri Bros Paving......157
Parc Olympique......46, 47
Paul Dry Books......32, 33
Peet's Coffee & Tea......159
Pernod Ricard......181
Portuguese Football Federation......27
"Red Bracer" production company......159
Regina Rubino / Robert Louey......130, 131
Risd Class of 2013......138
Rose Cole......160
Royal Volume......158
Saint Lucia Tourism Board......77
Sal. Oppenheim jr. & Cie.......110
School of Visual Arts......89, 193, 194
Seattle International Film Festival......197

Sisters......157
S Magazine......112, 113
Southcentre Mall......74, 75
Southwest Airlines......81
Stanley......44, 45
Stanley Kubrick Archive......206
Stars & Stripes Foundation......86, 87
St. Louis International Inc., SSC Limited......163, 164
Stokelj wines......175
Stranger & Stranger......165
Studio Hinrichs......84, 215
Sundance Construction......157
Tangerine (formerly ING Direct)......129
Teatr-Teatr theatrical center in Perm......199
Téléfilm Canada......66
Tenth and Page Realty......155
The Coca-Cola Company North America......171
The University of Hartford, Hartford Art School......24, 25
The University of Texas School of Architecture......208
Timberland......85
Touchstone Climbing......157
Truett Hurst......182
Turett Architect......160
Ultra Creative Client Gift......224, 225
Under Armour......145
Underline Studio......111, 183
UNICEF......26
University of Cincinnati (School of Design, Art, Architecture and Planning)......200
Upland Brewing Company......190, 191
Wallace Church, Inc.......147
Waller Creek Revitalization Initiative......160
Webster......223
Wednesday Seven......228, 229
Wells Fargo......78
Williams-Sonoma, Inc. (Mark and Graham)......58, 59
World Wildlife Fund......100-103
Yoav Gilat......150
Yumblebee......156

Winners Directory

PLATINUM WINNERS

beierarbeit www.beierarbeit.de
Sattelmeyerweg 1
33609 Bielefeld, Germany
Tel 49 521 787 1030
chb@beierarbeit.de

Faith www.faith.ca
622 Canyon Street
Mississauga, ON L5H 4L8 Canada
Tel 905 891 7410
info@faith.ca

Frost* Design
www.frostdesign.com.au
1/15 Foster Street, Surry Hills
Sydney, NSW 2010 Australia
Tel 61 2 9280 4233
info@frostdesign.com.au

Graham Hanson Design
www.grahamhanson.com
475 Park Ave
New York, NY 10016 United States
Tel 212 481 2858
info@grahamhanson.com

Headcase Design
www.headcasedesign.com
428 North 13th Street, 5F
Philadelphia, PA 19123 United States
Tel 215 922 5393
headcase@headcasedesign.com

IF Studio www.ifstudiony.com
670 Broadway Suite 301
New York, NY 10012 United States
Tel 212 334 3465
info@ifstudiony.com

Jan Sabach Design
www.krop.com/jansabach
Brooklyn, NY United States
Tel 718 310 8966
jan@sabach.cz

peter bankov
www.typographicposters.com
peter-bankov
p.bankov@designdepot.ru

Rebecca Bartlett LLC
www.rebeccabartlett.com
hello@rebeccabartlett.com

Toppan Printing Co., Ltd.
www.toppan.co.jp
1-1-3 Suido Bunkyo-ku
Tokyo 1128531 Japan
Tel 212 489 7740
mescal@mac.com

GOLD WINNERS

601 Design, Inc.
www.bruceholdeman.com
PO Box 771202
Steamboat Springs, CO 80477
United States
Tel 970 819 4264
bruce@601design.com

9 Threads www.9threads.com
8 W 38th St., New York, NY
10018 United States
Tel 646 278 1531
caroline.diaco@9threads.com

Addison www.addison.com
48 Wall Street
New York, NY 10005 United States
Tel 212 229 5000
info@addison.com

Apple www.apple.com
1 Infinite Loop
Cupertino, CA 95014 United States
Tel 408 996 1010

AS IF Media Group, LLC
www.asifmag.com
info@asifmag.com

Bailey Lauerman
www.baileylauerman.com
1299 Farnam Street, Suite 930
Omaha, NE 68102 United States
Tel 402 514 9400
jdoria@baileylauerman.com

BRED www.brednation.com
175 Claremont Ave, No. 66
New York, NY 10027 United States
Tel 212 861 8371
info@brednation.com

Chase Design Group
www.chasedesigngroup.com
220 East 23rd Street, Suite 600
New York, NY 10010 United States
Tel 212 660 2464
info_ny@chasedesigngroup.com

CP+B www.cpbgroup.com
3390 Mary Street, Suite 300
Coconut Grove, FL 33133 United States
Tel 305 859 2070
info@cpbgroup.com

Cue www.designcue.com
520 Nicollet Mall Suite 500
Minneapolis, MN 55402 United States
Tel 612 465 0030
info@designcue.com

Dankook University
www.dankook.ac.kr
152, Jukjeon-ro, Suji-gu
Yongin-si, Gyeonggi-do
448-701 Korea
Tel 82 1899 3700
letsdoit@dankook.ac.kr

Fellow www.fellowinc.com
2609 Aldrich Ave S 103
Minneapolis, MN
55408 United States
Tel 612 605 1712
kwolf@fellowinc.com

Founded by Design
www.foundedbydesign.com
Studio 501, 104 Commonwealth Street
Surry Hills, Sydney, NSW 2010 Australia
Tel 61 431 660 938
info@foundedbydesign.com

GQ www.gq.com
4 Times Square New York, NY
10036 United States
Tel 212 286 2860
info@gq.com

Hawkeye Communications
www.hawkeyecommunications.com
551 5th Ave
New York, NY 10176 United States
Tel 212 763 0200

HI(NY) Design www.hinydesign.com
401 Broadway 1908
New York, NY 10013 United States
Tel 646 808 0708
info@hinydesign.com

Hoyne www.hoyne.com.au
117 Reservoir Street
Surry Hills, NSW 2010 Australia
Tel 61 02 9212 2255
andrew@hoyne.com.au

IDEAS360° | SG360° a Segerdahl company
www.sg360.com
Tel 847 850 8912
mpantuso@sg360.com

Intellecta Corporate
www.intellectacorporate.se
Birger Jarlsgatan 57 B
Stockholm, Sweden
Tel 0 10 212 20 00
corporate@intellecta.se

KMD Inc. www.km-d.jp
info@km-d.jp

Landesberg Design
www.landesbergdesign.com
1219 Bingham St.
Pittsburgh, PA 15203
United States
Tel 412 381 2220
info@landesbergdesign.com

Landor Associates, Ohio
www.landor.com
110 Shillito Place
Cincinnati, OH 45202
United States
Tel 513 419 2300
hello@landor.com

Landor Associates, New York
www.landor.com
230 Park Ave S
New York, NY 10003
United States
Tel 888 252 6367
hello@landor.com

Laurie Frankel Photography
www.lauriefrankel.com
697 Douglass Street
San Francisco, CA
94114 United States
Tel 415 282 7345
info@lauriefrankel.com

lg2boutique
www.lg2boutique.com
585 Charest Blvd. East, 8th Floor
Québec, Québec
G1K3J2 Canada
Tel 418 263 8901
infogc@lg2.com

Lippincott www.lippincott.com
499 Park Ave New York,
NY 10022 United States
Tel 212 521 0000
info@lippincott.com

Liquid Agency
www.liquidagency.com
448 S. Market Street
San Jose, CA 95113
United States
Tel 408 850 8800
info@liquidagency.com

Lorenc+Yoo Design Inc
www.lorencyoodesign.com
109 Vickery Street
Roswell, GA 30075
United States
Tel 770 645 2828
jan@lorencyoodesign.com

Mason Zimbler www.mzl.com
9442 Capital of Texas Highway
Plaza 1, Suite 600
Austin, TX 78759 United States
Tel 866 228 2350
hello@mzl.com

Michael Schwab Studio
www.michaelschwab.com
108 Tamalpais Ave
San Anselmo, CA 94960
United States
Tel 415 257 5792
studio@michaelschwab.com

Morla Design
www.morladesign.com
1008A Pennsylvania Ave
San Francisco, CA 94107
United States
Tel 415 543 6548
info@morladesign.com

Nuno Duarte Martins
www.nunomartins.com
nuno@nunomartins.com

omdr Co.,Ltd.
www.omdr.co.jp
desk@omdr.co.jp

Parallax Design
www.parallaxdesign.com.au
123 Sturt Street
Adelaide, SA 5000 Australia
Tel 61 8 8410 8855
hello@paradoxdesign.com.au

Pentagram www.pentagram.com
1508 West Fifth Street
Austin, TX 78703
United States
Tel 512 476 3076
howdy@texas.pentagram.com

Peppermill Projects
www.peppermillprojects.com
102 Edgewood Ave.
Annapolis, MD 21401
United States
Tel 410 934 1073
hello@peppermillprojects.com

Piera Wolf www.pierawolf.ch
contact@pierawolf.ch

Poulin + Morris Inc.
www.poulinmorris.com
46 White Street, 2nd Floor
New York, NY 10013
United States
Tel 212 675 1332
info@poulinmorris.com

Raison Pure NYC
www.raisonpurenyc.com
119 5th Ave #2
New York, NY 10003
United States
Tel 212 625 0708
cmountain@raisonpureusa.com

Ralph Appelbaum Associates
www.raany.com
88 Pine St
New York, NY 10005
United States
Tel 212 334 8200
contact@raany.com

RM&CO www.rossimazzei.com
Studio 310 (The White Studios)
62 Templeton Street
Glasgow 640 1DA United Kingdom
uk@rossimazzei.com

Sagmeister & Walsh
www.sagmeisterwalsh.com
206 W 23rd Street, 4th Floor
New York, NY 10011
United States
Tel 212 647 1789
info@sagmeisterwalsh.com

Shadia Design
www.shadiadesign.com.au
207 The Parade Norwood
SA 5067 Australia
Tel 61 8 8332 9922
shadia@shadiadesign.com.au

Squires & Company
www.squirescompany.com
3624 Oak Lawn Ave
Dallas, TX 75219 United States
Tel 214 939 9194
info@squirescompany.com

Spela Draslar S.P.
Kadilnikova 1 Ljubljana Sl
spela.draslar@siol.net

Stranger & Stranger
www.strangerandstranger.com
42 Greene Street, 5th Floor
New York, NY 10013
United States
Tel 212 625 2441

Studio 32 North
www.studio32north.com
3315 Thorn Street
San Diego, CA 92104 United States
Tel 415 613 4136
sallie@studio32north.com

Studio Hinrichs
www.studio-hinrichs.com
368 Clementina St.
San Francisco, CA 94103
United States
Tel 415 546 1380
info@studio-hinrichs.com

Sydney Rogers, LLC
www.sydneyrogersland.com
3 E 54th Street, Ste. 900
New York, NY 10022
United States
sydney@sydneyrogersland.com

Taxi Studio Ltd
www.taxistudio.co.uk
93 Princess Victoria St.
Bristol BS8 4DD, United Kingdom
Tel 44 117 973 5151
fearless@taxistudio.co.uk

Turner Duckworth: London
www.turnerduckworth.com
Voysey House
Barley Mow Passage
London W4 4PH United Kingdom
Tel 44 0 20 8994 7190
cat@turnerduckworth.co.uk

Turner Duckworth: San Francisco
www.turnerduckworth.com
831 Montgomery Street
San Francisco, CA 94133 United States
Tel 415 675 7777
amy@turnerduckworth.com

Visual Arts Press, Ltd. www.sva.edu
209 E 23rd St. New York,
NY 10010 United States
Tel 212 592 2000
vap@sva.edu

Webster Design
www.websterdesign.com
5060 Dodge St.
Omaha, NE 68132 United States
Tel 402 551 0503
info@websterdesign.com

Weymouth Design
www.weymouthdesign.com
332 Congress Street, Floor 6
Boston, MA 02210 United States
Tel 617 542 2647
info@weymouthdesign.com

WONGDOODY www.wongdoody.com
10011 Western Ave Seattle,
WA 98104 United States
Tel 206 624 5325

WPA Pinfold
www.wpa-pinfold.co.uk
33 Cavendish Square
London W1G OPW
United Kingdom
Tel 44 0 20 7436 9219
elaine@wpa-pinfold.co.uk

Winners Directory

160over90 www.160over90.com
One South Broad Street, 10th Floor
Philadelphia, PA 19107 United States
Tel 215 732 3200
newbusiness@160over90.com

21xdesign www.21xdesign.com
2713 S. Kent Rd. Broomall PA
19008 United States
Tel 610 325 5422

9 Threads www.9threads.com
8 W 38th Street New York,
NY 10018 United States
Tel 646 278 1531
caroline.diaco@9threads.com

AG Creative www.agcreative.ca
4710 Kingswway Suite 2129
Burnaby, BC V5H 4M2
Tel 604 559 1411

Alt Group www.altgroup.net
16-18 Mackelvie Street, Grey Lunn
PO Box 47873 Ponsonby 114
Auckland, New Zealand
Tel 64 9 360 3910
info@altgroup.net

Arcana Academy
www.arcanaacademy.com
13323 Washington Blvd. Ste 301
Los Angeles, CA 90066
United States
Tel 310 279 5024
info@arcanaacademy.com

Ayşe Çelem Design
www.ayşeçelemdesign.com
Arnavutköy 1. Cadde 89 Besiktas
Istanbul 34345 Turkey
Tel 90 212 358 20 93
ayse@ayşeçelemdesign.com

BEAMY www.wearebeamy.com
49 Fuxing West Road No. 4
Unit 101, Xuhui District
Shanghai 200031 China
Tel 86 21 5423 3675
hello@wearebeamy.com

Brand Union www.thebrandunion.com
3 Columbus Circle, 11th Floor
New York, NY 10019 United States
Tel 212 336 3200
newyork@brandunion.com

Brand Union www.thebrandunion.com
11-33 St John Street London,
EC1M 4AA United Kingdom
Tel 44 207 559 7000
london@brandunion.com

Chase Design Group
www.chasedesigngroup.com
220 E 23rd Street, Suite 600
New York, NY 10010 United States
Tel 212 660 2464
info_ny@chasedesigngroup.com

Concrete Design Communications Inc.
www.concrete.ca
2 Silver Ave Toronto,
ON M6R 3A2 Canada
Tel 416 534 9960
mail@concrete.ca

Connelly Partners / ISMCP
www.connellypartners.com
46 Waltham Street 4thy Floor
Boston, MA 02118 United States
Tel 617 521 5400
jvogt@connellypartners.com

Craig-Teerlink Design
430 Day Street, San Francisco,
CA 94131 United States
Tel 415 821 9591

DAE www.dae.com
71 Stevenson Street Suite 750
San Francisco, CA 94105
United States
Tel 415 341 1280

Design is Play www.designisplay.com
855 Folsom Street, 931
San Francisco, CA 94107
United States
Tel 415 505 6242
studio@designisplay.com

The Designory www.designory.com
211 East Ocean Blvd., Ste. 100
Long Beach, CA 90802
United States
Tel 562 624 0200

Dessein www.dessein.com.au
130 Aberdeen Street
Northbridge
Perth Western Australia
Tel 089 228 0661
geoff@dessein.com.au

DNA dna.co.nz
Level 2, 262 Thorndon Quay
PO Box 3056 Thorndon
Wellington 6140 New Zealand
Tel 04 499 0828
zn.oc.and@trub.hsoj

Dyal and Partners dyalpartners.com
1801 Lavaca St #115
Austin, TX 78701 United States
Tel 512 8103311
info@dyalpartners.com

Flake flake.fi
Kortesuonkatu 51
Jyväskylä 40700 Finland
info@flake.fi

The General Design Co.
www.generaldesignco.com
1624 Q St NW
Washington, DC 20009
United States
Tel 202 640 1842
hello@generaldesignco.com

GQ www.gq.com
4 Times Square New York,
NY 10036 United States
Tel 212 286 2860
info@gq.com

H.Tuncay Design
Omerrustupasa Sokak
Birlik Apt. 26/8 Besiktas
Istanbul, Turkey

Hawkeye Communications
www.hawkeyecommunications.com
10575 Westoffice Drive Houston,
TX 77042 United States
Tel 713 783 8844
info@hawkeyecommunications.com

HOOK www.hookusa.com
522 King St. Charleston,
SC 29403 United States
Tel 843 853 5532
info@hookusa.com

HUSH Studios www.heyhush.com
68 Jay Street, Suite 413
Brooklyn, NY 11201
Jersey City, NJ 07302
United States
Tel 718 422 1537
jake@hustleandcompany.com

HY Connect www.hyc.com
1000 North Water Street, Suite 1600
Milwaukee, WI 53202 United States
Tel 414 225 9534
tpeterson@hyc.com

INNOCEAN USA
www.innoceanusa.com
180 5th Street #200
Huntington Beach, CA 92648
United States
Tel 714 861 5200
info@innoceanusa.com

Interbrand
www.interbrand.com
4000 Smith Road Cincinnati,
OH 45209 United States
Tel 877 692 7263
inquiries@interbrand.com

KEI TAKIMOTO
Tokyo, Japan
keitakimoto.work@gmail.com

KMD Inc. www.km-d.jp
info@km-d.jp

Landor Associates www.landor.com
1001 Front Street
San Francisco, CA 94111
United States
Tel 415 365 1700
hello@ landor.com

Leap www.leapwith.us
45 Bromfield St 11th Floor
Boston, MA 02108
United States
Tel 617 721 7749

Leynivopnid www.leynivopnid.is
Solvallagata 66 101
Reykjavik, Iceland
Tel 354 840 0220
einar@leynivopnid.is

lg2boutique ww.lg2boutique.com
3575 Saint-Laurent Blvd., Suite 900
Montréal Québec H2X 2T7
Tel 514 281 0957
info.boutique@lg2.com

Liquid Agency www.liquidagency.com
448 S. Market Street San Jose,
CA 95113 United States
Tel 408 850 8800
info@liquidagency.com

McCann Detroit
www.mccanndetroit.com
360 W Maple Rd. Birmingham, MI
48009 United States
Tel 248 203 8000
mike.crone@mccann.com

Mermaid, Inc. www.mermaidnyc.com
41 Union Square West
New York, NY 10003
United States
Tel 212 337 0707
sharon@mermaidnyc.com

Michael Schwab Studio
www.michaelschwab.com
108 Tamalpais Ave
San Anselmo, CA 94960
United States
Tel 415 257 5792
studio@michaelschwab.com

MiresBall www.miresball.com
2605 State Street San Diego
CA 92103 United States
Tel 619 234 6631
julie@miresball.com

mkcreative mkanyc.com
16 West 22nd Street, 3rd Floor
New York, NY 10010
United States
Tel 212 367 9225
info@mkanyc.com

Monogram www.monogram.com
L2A 119 Kippax Street Surry Hills
NSW 2010 Australia
Tel 61 02 8004 6423
mgm@monogramdesign.com

NONOBJECT www.nonobject.com
853 Alma Street, Palo Alto, CA
94301 United States
Tel 650 473 9040
info@nonobject.com

Odear www.odear.se
112 24 Stockholm Sweden
Tel 46 70 738 2101
contact@odear.se

The Office of Gilbert Li
www.gilbertli.com
777 Richmond St W #2027
Toronto, ON M6J 0C2 Canada
Tel 416 979 7582
office@gilbertli.com

The Partners www.the-partners.com
75 Spring Street,2nd Floor
New York, NY 10012 United States
Tel 917 946 2104
claire@the-partners.com

Pentagram www.pentagram.com
1508 West Fifth Street
Austin, TX 78703 United States
Tel 512 476 3076
howdy@texas.pentagram.com

Peter Schmidt Group
www.peter-schmidt-group.de
Grünstraße 15 40212
Düsseldorf Germany
Tel 49 0 211 30102 0
info@peter-schmidt-group.de

Poulin + Morris Inc.
www.poulinmorris.com
46 White Street, Second Floor
New York, NY 10013 United States
Tel 212 675 1332
info@poulinmorris.com

Publicis Kaplan Thaler
www.kaplanthaler.com
1675 Broadway New York,
NY 10019 United States
Tel 212 474 5000
matthew.anderson@pkt.com

Regina Rubino / Robert Louey
2525 Main St #204
Santa Monica, CA 90405
United States
Tel 310 998 8898
reginarubino@imageglobalvision

Rhode Island School of Design
www.risd.edu
2 College Street, Providence
RI 02903 United States
Tel 401 454 610
info@risd.edu

Rice Creative
www.behance.net/Rice_Creative
info@ricecreative.com

The Rivalry www.therivalry.co
NYC 10014 United States
inquire@therivalry.co

Shamlian Creative
www.shamliancreative.com
Tel 610 892 0570
info@open-inc.com

SID LEE sidlee.com
75 Queen Street, Office 1400
Montréal, Québec H3C 2N6 Canada
Tel 514 282 2200
info@sidlee.com

SMOG Design, Inc.
www.smogdesign.com
1725 Silver Lake Boulevard
Los Angeles, CA 90026
United States
Tel 323 668 9073
mail@smogdesign.com

Steven Taylor Associates
www.steventaylorassociates.com
317 The Plaza 535 King's Rd
London SW10 0SZ United Kingdom
Tel 44 20 7351 2345
info@steventaylorassociates.com

Stranger & Stranger
www.strangerandstranger.com
42 Greene Street, 5th Floor
New York, NY 10013
United States
Tel 212 625 2441

Studio Hinrichs
www.studio-hinrichs.com
368 Clementina Street
San Francisco, CA 94103
United States
Tel 415 546 1380
info@studio-hinrichs.com

Subplot Design Inc.
www.subplot.com
318 Homer Street, Suite 301
Vancouver, BC V6A 1B2Canada
Tel 1 604 685 2990
info@subplot.com

Sumo www.sumodesign.co.uk
Sumo, 71 Westgate Road
Newcastle upon Tyne, NE1 1SG
United Kingdom
Tel 0191 261 9894
info@sumodesign.co.uk

Timberland In-House www.vfc.com
105 Corporate Center Blvd
Greensboro, NC 27408 United States
Tel 336 424 6000
info@vfc.com

TOKY toky.com
3001 Locust Street St Louis,
MO 63103 United States
Tel 314 534 2000
info@toky.com

Toolbox Design
www.toolboxdesign.com
403-1228 Hamilton Street
Vancouver BC
V6B 6L2 Canada
Tel 604 739 9932
info@toolboxdesign.com

Turner Duckworth Design: London
www.turnerduckworth.com
Voysey House Barley Mow Passage
London W4 4PH United Kingdom
Tel 44 0 20 8994 7190

Ultra Creative www.ultracreative.com
43 Main Street SE, Suite 430
Minneapolis, MN 55414
United States
Tel 612 378 0748
info@ultracreative.com

Underline Studio
www.underlinestudio.com
247 Wallace Ave, 2nd Floor
Toronto, Ontario Canada M6H 1V5
Tel 416 341 0475
info@underlinestudio.com

University of Wisconsin--Green Bay
www.uwgb.edu
2420 Nicolet Dr. Green Bay,
WI 54311 United States
Tel 920 465 2000
uwgb@uwgb.edu

Wallace Church
www.wallacechurch.com
330 E 48th St #1
New York, NY 10017 United States
Tel 212 755 2903
info@wallacechurch.com

The White Room Inc
www.thewhiteroom.ca
191 1st Ave Toronto
Canada M4M 1X3
Tel 416 901 7736
info@thewhiteroom.ca

White Studio www.whitestudio.com
Rua Alexandre Braga, 94 — 1.° E
4000-049 Porto, Portugal
Tel 351 22 616 90 80
mail@whitestudio.pt

WPA Pinfold
www.wpa-pinfold.co.uk
33 Cavendish Square
London W1G OPW
United Kingdom
Tel 44 0 20 7436 9219
elaine@wpa-pinfold.co.uk

xose teiga, studio.
www.behance.net/XoseTeiga
Av de Rodríguez de Viguri, 31
15703 Santiago de Compostela
La Coruña, Spain
Tel 34 607 15 52 11

Young & Laramore www.yandl.com
407 Fulton Street, Indianapolis,
IN 46202 United States
Tel 317 264 8000
tdenari@yandl.com

Zulu Alpha Kilo www.zulualphakilo.com
260 King St E b101 Toronto,
ON M5A 4L5 Canada
Tel 416 777 9858
INeedANewAgency@zulualphakilo.com

Winners by Country

BEST IN THE AMERICAS

CANADA 🇨🇦

AG Creative......................................157
Concrete Design Communication....129,
....219
CP+B...189
Faith...104-106
Ig2boutique........42, 43, 46, 47, 50, 51, 66
The Office of Gilbert Li..................54, 55
SID LEE..188
Subplot Design Inc............................234
Toolbox Design.....................74, 75, 158
Underline Studio.......................111, 183
The White Room Inc.................117, 146
Zulu Alpha Kilo.................................209

USA 🇺🇸

160over90......................................24, 25
21xdesign......................................32, 33
601 Design, Inc........................203, 204
9Threads.................................115, 116
Addison...22, 23
Apple..186
Arcana Academy................................64
ASIF Media Group, LLC................107-109
Bailey Lauerman...............................156
Brand Union......................................181
BRED...218
Chase Design Group.................160, 168
Connelly Partners / ISMCP..................77
Craig-Teerlink Design........................157
Cue...180
DAE...78, 81
Design is Play........................155, 157
The Designory................................72, 73
Dyal and Partners.............................208
Fellow...41, 148
The General Design Co..........155, 159
GQ...92-99
Graham Hanson Design....................152
Hawkeye Communications.......157, 174
Headcase Design............................28, 29

HI(NY) Design..........................163, 164
HOOK...158
HUSH Studios...................................145
HY Connect...............................226, 227
IDEAS360°.............68, 69, 139, 140
IF Studio........68, 69, 201, 202, 205, 216
INNOCEAN USA......................141, 143
Interbrand...................56, 57, 221, 222
Jan Sabach Design...........................192
Landesberg Design...........................161
Landor Associates........67, 166, 167, 200
Laurie Frankel Photography.............214
Leap...160
Lippincott....38, 39, 44, 45, 48, 49, 134, 135
Liquid Agency...........................155, 169
Lorenc+Yoo Design Inc...........126, 127
Mason Zimbler.................................144
McCann Detroit.................................178
Mermaid, Inc.....................................155
Michael Schwab Studio............150, 159
MiresBall..185
mkcreative..160
Morla Design................................58, 59
NONOBJECT.......................212, 220
The Partners....................................151
Pentagram.......36, 37, 100-103, 114, 160
Peppermill Projects..........................150
Poulin + Morris Inc.................118, 119,
.............................124, 125, 132, 133
Publicis Kaplan Thaler................60, 61
Raison Pure NYC.............................170
Ralph Appelbaum Associates..136, 137
Rebecca Bartlett LLC...............228, 229
Regina Rubino / Robert Louey...130, 131
Risd Class of 2013............................138
The Rivalry.............................152, 153
Sagmeister & Walsh..............193, 194
Shamlian Creative...........................154
SMOG Design, Inc...................30, 31
Squires & Company..........................156
Stranger & Stranger......165, 173, 182
Studio 32 North................................177

Studio Hinrichs.............84, 86, 87, 215
Sydney Rogers, LLC................210, 211
Timberland In-House..........................85
TOKY.......................................230, 231
Turner Duckworth Design: London &
San Francisco...................................171
Ultra Creative...........................224, 225
University of Wisconsin-Green Bay...142
Visual Arts Press, Ltd..........89, 193, 194
Wallace Church, Inc...........................147
Webster.......................223, 232, 233
Weymouth Design.............................217
WONGDOODY...............................197
Young & Laramore...................190, 191

BEST IN EUROPE & AFRICA

CZECH REPUBLIC 🇨🇿

peter bankov.....................................199

FINLAND 🇫🇮

Flake...159

GERMANY 🇩🇪

beierarbeit..184
Peter Schmidt Group.........................110

ICELAND 🇮🇸

Leynivopnid......................................157

SWEDEN 🇸🇪

Intellecta Corporate...................20, 21
Odear..155

SWITZERLAND 🇨🇭

Piera Wolf.................................112, 113

PORTUGAL 🇵🇹

Nuno Duarte Martins...........................27
White Studio................................34, 35

SPAIN 🇪🇸

xose teiga, studio.............................160

UNITED KINGDOM 🇬🇧

Brand Union...........................179, 181
Landor Associates.............................206
RM&CO...162

Steven Taylor Associates.....................76
Sumo..235
Taxi Studio Ltd..................................176
Turner Duckworth:
London & San Francisco...................187
WPA Pinfold............40, 52, 53, 90, 91

SLOVENIA 🇸🇮

Spela Draslar S.P..............................175

BEST IN ASIA & OCEANIA

AUSTRALIA 🇦🇺

Dessein...88
Founded by Design..............................65
Frost* Design.........................195, 196
Hoyne...70, 71
Monogram...149
Parallax Design.......................122, 123
Shadia Design.............................62, 63

CHINA 🇨🇳

BEAMY..83

SOUTH KOREA 🇰🇷

Dankook University...........................198

JAPAN 🇯🇵

KEI TAKIMOTO...............................236
KMD Inc....................120, 121, 128
omdr Co.,Ltd.....................................207
Toppan Printing Co., Ltd........79, 80

NEW ZEALAND 🇳🇿

Alt Group..155
DNA..213

VIETNAM 🇻🇳

Rice Creative..............................26, 172

TURKEY 🇹🇷

Ayşe Çelem Design.............................82
H.Tuncay Design...............................159

Visit graphis.com to view top design work within each Country, State or Province.

All Entrants

Abbot, Rodney
Abrams, J.J.
Adair, Ryan
Adams, Gayle
Aftimos, Nadia
Ahmed, Sana
Ahrens, Justin
Aires, Eduardo
Alexander, Rob
Alias Adi, Hagit
Allen, Melissa
Allen, Sallie Reynolds
Amador, Jorge
Amann, Lesley
Ambler, Jamie
Amborn, Jesse
An, Sang
Ancalmo, Carlos
Anderson, Elizabeth
Andersson, Daniel
Andersson, Jonas
Annbjer, Daniel
Annesanti, Monica
Antipas, Anna-Marie
Aoyagi, Masahiro
Apple Marketing
  Communications
Aprea, Michelle
Arakawa, Chie
Arango, Kyle
Archbold, Roger
Ardzivian, Ani
Arends, Kate
Arias, Phil
Arias, Philip
Arky, David
Armer, Heather
Arnold, Zach
Arriaza, Jon
Arzoo, Derek
Ash, Greg
Atkin, John
Atkin, Trudi
Atkinson, Ryan
au Williams, Rebecca
Au, Simon
Auchu, Claude
Aurilio, Valerie
Ayling, Sam
Azevedo, Athena
Babich, Oleg
Baca, Elena
Baccari, Alberto
Bae, Jinny
Bailey, Ryan
Balbarin, John
Balen, Leanne
Balint, Martin-Emilian
Ball, Jimmy
Ball, John
Bankov, Peter
Banton, Brian
Barcellona, Luca
Barratt, Matt
Barrett, Aidan
Barrett, Howard
Barter, Jared
Bartlett, Rebecca
Bartolo, Domenic
Baruchin, Uri
Baskin, Anya
Bateman, James
Batisz, Miklós
Bayne, Bill
Beatty, Shawn
Beaulieu, Mike
Beckwith, Dana
Beers, Sue
Beier, Christoph
Bell, Patsy Ann
Bellini, Kelly
Belser, Burkey
Berger, Nichole
Beurskens, Mia
Bickford, Geoff
Bierwirth, Andreas
Billqvist, Henrik
Black, Elizabeth
Blackmore, Casey
Blakemore, David
Blau, Christian
Blevins, Webb
Blockley, Simon
Bloom, Ben
Bloom, Gary
Boesch, Nina
Bofill, Mooren
Bolter, Miranda
Bonfig, Jessica
Booth, Ryan
Börsting, Robert
Boske, Karl-Magnus
Bothwell, Amanda

Bott, Luke
Boud, Jamie
Bourdon, Catherine
Bours, Benjamin
Bowers, Amanda
Bowsher, Ben
Boyd, Eric
Boyd, Matthew
Braceros, Nathan
Bradbury, Catharine
Braley, Michael
Braun, Greg
Breidenbach, Joshua
Breininger, Brad
Bresler, Patti
Brickell, Caroline
Brickell, Carrie
Brignell, Ian
Brindley, Dan
Briscoe, Andy
Brittain, Michael
Broad, Louise
Brooks, Tyler
Brown, Mark
Brown, Natalie
Brown, Travis
Brue, Nick
Bryant, Karin
Buhrman Jr., Jim
Bunny, Paula
Burckhardt, Marc
Burfitt, Lovisa
Burgess, Duane
Burkhart, Bryan
Burns, William
Bussolati, Monica
Butler, Cameron
Byrnes, Samuel
Cabral, Luciana
Calcao, Tony
Cambronero, Jinki
Campbell, Cosmo
Campbell, Jean
Campbell, Nancy
Cárdenas, Johnny
Cardinal, Chelsea
Carl, Matthew
Carrasquilla, Santiago
Carrillo, Andreina
Carter, Katie
Carvalho, Flavio
Cast, Christopher
Castelletti, Andrea
Cates, Whitney
Catterson, Mark
Cech, Jay
Cehovin, Edward
Çelem, Ayşe
Ceo, Marco
Cervantes, Andrei
Chambers, J
Chan, Gloria
Chan, Jennifer
Chandler, Ross
Chang, Frances
Charter, Ellie
Chase, Margo
Chatham, Cody
Chau, Janson
Chavez, Melissa
Chen, A.Y.
Chen, Eran
Cherico, Kathy Chia
Chernock, Melanie
Cheung, Hera
Chew, Jimmy
Chew, Susan
Chi-Lung, Calvin, Chan
Chiang, Kelvin
Chin, Conrad
Chiu, Andrew
Cho, Wendy
Cho, Yong Joon
Chock, Paul
Choi, Yosub Jack
Chu, Cindy
Chung, Hoon-Dong
Chung, Woo
Church, Stan
Cieciora, Tana
Cilli, Darryl
Clark, David
Clark, Don
Clark, Matthew
Clark, Nick
Clark, Randy
Clarke, Dan
Clarke, Martin
Clarke, Rob
Cleland, Grant
Clemente, Elton
Clodfelter, Ross
Coburn, Jim

Cochran, Kay
Coffey, Dustin
Colangelo, Robin
Colbourne, Richard
Coleman, Lauren
Coleman, Mark
Collins, Jamie
Collinsworth, Grant
Colvin, Alan
Comboy, Matt
Conerly, Wil
Connolly, Andrew
Conrick, Cherise
Coomber, Lee
Coonrod, Matt
Corea, Nicole
Corenswet, John
Cornell, Nikolai
Costin, Molly
Côté, Serge
Craig-Teerlink, Jean
Craig, Emily
Creamer, Alex
Crickman, Molly
Crookshank, Robyn
Crouchman, Ryan
Cruz, Antonio
Culpepper, Jennifer
Cunningham, Scott
Curley, Morgan
Dalton, Craig
Damitz, Tim
Danko, Mike
Dannenfelser, Scott
Darby, Keith
Darty, Jeremy
Dawson, Claire
De Leo, Chi-An
Decker, Darla
Deer, Adam
Deetz, Kristy
Delevant, Bob
Delevante, Bob
Delgado, Carla
Deluca, Anthony
DeLuise, Brooke
Demassi, Tali
Derksen, Joel
deVallance, Brendan
Devlin-Driskel, Patty
Devlin, Stewart
Diaz, Fabian
Dickerson, Dic
Dinh Thi Thuy, Truc
Distler, Joshua
Dixon, Brian
Dixon, Judy
Donovan, Anthony
Donovan, Bil
Dor, Yotam
Dorst, Doug
Doskocil, Andrea
Downey, Gavin
Downie, Alana
Drabb, Danny
Draper, Bekki
Draslar, Spela
Drew, Ned
Dry, Paul
Drymalski, Tom
Du Plessis, Jean
Duarte Martins, Nuno
Duckworth, Bruce
Dugas, Matt
Dunbar, Austin
Dunn, Troy
Dunstan-Brown, Phil
Duran, Lorena
Dvir, David
Dwyer, Nate
Dyal and Partners
Dyal, Herman
Dyer, Jimmy
Dyne, Greg
Dyson, Brandon
Eagleton, Nick
Edmondson, James
Edwards, Aaron
Edwards, Bruce
Elder, Paul
Elias Adi, Hagit
Elixir Design
Elkins, Kate
Elkouby, Ari
Elliot, Louise
Ellis, Justin
Emers, Kylie
Engqvist, Kornelia
Epstein, Lisa
Ericsdottir, Maria
E en, Sibel
Espersen, Angela
Espinoza, Dave

Esseveld, Alex
Euba, Javier
Ewald, Dave
Faden, Sean
Fairley, John
Farkas, Anna
Feakins, Rob
Feavel, Michael
Fedeles, Zoe
Felton, Mark
Feng, Sha
Ferrino, Marc
Feyerer, Julie
Filby, Jeff
Finco, Robin
Finke, Romy
Fiore, Carlo
Fishkind, Scott
Flores, Frankie
Folkerth, Beth
Ford, Rachel
Forkert, Clea
Foster, Amy
Fox, Lucy
Fox, Mark
Fox, Nathan
Fraga, Bruna
Frankel, Laurie
Frazier, Craig
Fredricks, Kathya
Frenkle, Julia
Frith, Robert
Froetscher, Walter
Frost, Vince
Fry, Barett
Fry, Barrett
Fuller, Alex
Fuller, Craig
Fullick, Hsu-Ying
Gabbert, Sarah
Gabor, Antonia
Gallop, Ben
Galvin, Akira
Gandy, Matt
Garcia, Kori
Gardner, Jeff
Gardner, Sam
Garofalo, Joelle
Garrett, Jenny
Garvey, Chris
Gast, Bradley
Gast, Jane
Gatterden, Diane
Gatti, Camilla
Gatti, Gemma
Gauthier, Nolan
Geana, Bogdan
Gee, Earl
Gehard, Thibault
Geiser, Chris
George, Carey
Georgiou, Pete
German, Geoff
Geroni, Ralph
Gerstner, Charles
Gertz, Mike
Gibbons, Stephanie
Gil, Aniela
Gilbert, Marie-Pier
Giles, Ellen
Gislason, Thorleifur
Glock, Remy
Glover, Patrick
Goad, Taylor
Goldberg, Barney
Golwitzer, Mary
Gomes, Gabi
Gonsalves, Dana
Gonzalez, Ana
Goodis, Codi
Goolsby, Clark
Goralnick, Steph
Goralnick, Stephanie
Gorgo, Mike
Granger, Gus
Grantham, Matt
Gray, Ben
Graziani, Francesco
Griffin, Chip
Grimsley, Rick
Gross, Sig
Guerin, Michael
Gunderson, Grant
Gunderson, Will
Gutin, JoAnn
Gylfason, Elnar
Habig, Jenna
Hackley, Will
Hadley, Kenta
Hadley, Sam
Hadlock, Carolyn
Hainaut, Laurent

Haire, Lauren
Halbur, Ted
Halderman, Lauri
Hale, Alison
Halford, Carl
Hall, Sam
Halpin, Clem
Hammond, Ryan
Hampton, Tyler
Hanjani, Ucef
Hans, Brianne
Hans, Wiliam
Hansanugrum, Paula
Hansen, Jon
Hansen, Karen
Hanson, Graham
Hardin, Nate
Hardy, Amy
Hardy, Tara
Hargis, Jason
Harrison, Dylan
Hart, Dale
Hartford, JB
Hartford, Jen
Hartford, Tim
Hartley, Helen
Hartono, Beverly
Hartung, Katja
Harvey, David
Haslag, Lydia
Hawthorne, Gary
Hayden, John
He, Sophia
Heard, Eugene
Heideke, Eduardo
Heinert, Loucinda
Heisler, Sean
Hennessy, Benjamin
Heptinstall, Greg
Herberg, Erik
Herbst, Scot
Hernandez, Ed
Herter, Erik
Hessel, Adam
Hester, Cassie
Heughens, Todd
Hiek, Gloria
Hill, Matthew
Hinkel, Jack
Hinkelbein, Gerrit
Hinrichs, Kit
Hinz, Nathan
Hische, Jessica
Ho, Lynn
Hoelter, Cam
Hoffman, Erin
Hoffman, Jay
Hoffpauir, Tim
Hogan, Christina
Hohmann, Marc
Holdeman, Bruce
Holmes, Patrick
Holmgeirsson, Jon Helgi
Holohan, Kelly
Holt, Brian
Homack, Robert
Horn, Kathy
Hosking, Glen
Hosokawa, Natsuko
Houk, Holly
Howry, Jill
Hoyne, Andrew
Huang, Swin
Huang, Wen Ping
Hubacek, Greg
Huber, Noah
Hudder, Thomas
Hurst, Richard
Hush, Tara
Hutchison, Scott
Huynh Tran Khanh,
  Nguyen
Hyde, Debbie
Iadanza, Patrick
Ide, Hisa
Ide, Kumiko
Ide, Toshiaki
Ikin, Zoe
Ilich, Stjepan
Ingram, Heather
Irlbeck, Brenda
Irvin, Thomas
Izuhara, Scott
Jackson, Steve
Jallick, Shane
Jariya, Jade
Jasinowski, Jeff
Jaxybai, Aika
Jennings, Christopher
Jesse, Greg
Johnson, Justin

Johnson, Mike
Johnston, Daniel
Johnstone, Jamie
Jointe, Andre
Joly, Aurelie
Jones, Dylan
Jones, Kristi
Jones, Marie
Jones, Tim
Joo, Evangeline
Jouflas, Susan
Judd, Peter
Judkins, Bryan
Jue, Desiree
Jue, San
Jung, Stewart
Kaczmarek, Jesse
Kagiwada, Paul
Kamran, Nadia
Kang, Michelle
Kapetanovic, Nino
Karasyk, Erik
Kato, Mayumi
Katona, Diti
Kayal, Brad
Kearney, Ali
Keeton, Wes
Kelley, Maren
Kemnitz, Lauren
Kendrick, Shane
Kennedy, Mark
Kenworthy, Tracy
Kepple, Paul
Kerns, Ashley
Kessous, David
Kew, Kate
Khouri, Omar
Khoury, Tarek
Killinger, Dana
Kim, Hea
Kim, Sung Yong
King, Sheila
Kinniburgh, Truda
Kinslow, Zack
Kirby, Ken
Kittle, Alan
kiyoung, AN
Kline, Chris
Kline, Katherine
Klix, Anea
Knapp, Peter
Knutson, Garth
Koch, Claus
Koenderink, Gerhard
Kostadinov, Kostadin
Kotulka, Jim
Koukodimos, Tom
Kowaleczko, Natalia
Kowledge, Trew
Kramer, Melissa
Krantz, Wally
Kraszewski, Robert
Kratschmer, Jeff
Kress, Doug
Kriefski, Michael
Krivicich, Robert
Krstic, Goran
Krull, John
Kubel, Henrik
Kuga, Steph
Kuga, Stephanie
Kulp, Thorsten
Kwok, Ben
Kwon, Bogdan
Kwon, Jinhee
Kwon, Jung
Labus, Brian
LaFontaine, Justin
Lai, Wai Kwan Gideon
Lakloufi, Greg
Lam, Frankie
Lam, Geoffrey
Lam, Gigi
Lam, Ping
Lan, Chloe
Lan, Kevin
Landesberg, Rick
Laneve, Giuseppe
Lang, Adam
Lange, Ulrich
Langer, Jason
Lanz, Tracey
Larivee, April
Larsen, Imri
Laursen, Gina
lau, wing
Laube, Bart
Lawrence, Steve
Lawton, Bradford
Lays, Julie
Ledgerwood, Mark
Lee, Bryan

Lee, Christopher
Lee, Dean
Lee, Dexter
Lee, Esther
Lee, Heather
Lee, Ken-tsai
Lee, Ronn
Lehmann, Christopher
Lescarbeau, Maude
Leung, Skye
Leung, Wai Shing
Lewis, Tom
Li, Gilbert
Lin, Chun-Ying
Lindstedt, Mattias
Linkugel, Kris
Linskill, Jeremy
Liong, Karen
Lipman, Steve
Little, Adam
Little, Jason
Liu, Mac
Liversidge, Romy
Livingston, Judy
Lo, Oliver
Loboda, Karolina
Lockaby, Brandy
Logan, Cris
Loglisci, Karin
Looney, Butler
Lorenc, Jan
Louey, Robert
Louie, Bryan
Louie, Wes
LPL Financial Research
Luba, Roman
Luc, An
Ludwig, Travis
Lugenbuehl, Mark
Lukic, Branko
Lukic, Suncica
Luong, Jenny
Lurcock, Matt
Ly, An
Ly, David
Lynch, Jason
Lyons, Steven
Mabry, Kiley
Mac Cormack, Dermot
Machado, Graziela
Mackay, Kala
MacKenzie, Lynne
Macknight Dearborn, Kari
Madison, Kipp
Madlem, Andy
Maegawa, Junko
Maher, Craig
Mai Ngoc Que, Lan
Maierhofer, Knut
Maldonado, Luigi
Malsy, Monika
Mao, Dominique
Marceau, Bill
Margaritis, George
Marin, John
Marinovich, Erik
Märki, Patrick
Marois, Marilyn
Marroquin, Elda
Marshall, Ben
Marshall, Miles
Martin, Alyssa
Martinson Davis, JoEllen
Maruyama, Misako
Mastrion, Guy
Matauch, Dan
Matthews, Emily
Mattson, Eric
Matzke, Michael
Maurer, Jeff
Mayers, Crystal
Mays, Aaron
McCall, Cory
McCall, Steve
McCandliss, Trevett
McCarthy, Angela
McClure, Derek
McCluskey, Sue
McCormick, Michael
McCoy, Justin
McCoy, Terry
McDermott, Joe
McElroy, Patricia
McGinness, Will
Mclaughlin, Sharon
McMahon, Chris
McMaster, Jennifer
McNamara, Andrew
Meddin, Maryam
Medrano, Henry
Meers, Katie
Mendez, Manuel
Meng, Hope

All Entrants

Merino, Steve
Meyer, John
Michael Schwab Studio
Michaud, Bruno
Michels, Josh
Middleton, Morgan
Mikin, David
Miles, Bryan
Miller, Chad
Miller, Kristen
Miller, Tom
Milton 2, Roy
Minini, Marcos
Minkin, David
Miranda, Prashant
Mires, Scott
Misawa, Osamu
Mitchell, Jamie
Miyazaki, Kei
Mizrachi, Efrat
Moehler, Michelle
Moffat, Sarah
Moll, Justin
Monahan, Jeff
Mondes de Oca, Leonor
Mondor, Philip
Montes, Chemi
Montesca, Lia
Morales, Daniel
Morales, Esther
Morcos, Wael
Mordasky, Tom
Morey, Stuart
Moriel, Polina
Morla, Jennifer
Morren, Jamie
Moua, Nipon
Mouland, Virginia
Mroueh, Zac
Mroueh, Zak
Muckenthaler, Scott
Mui, Kai
Mumpower, Alison
Muñoz, Albert
Muñoz, John
Murray, Brandon
Murray, Dean
Nadaskay, Amy
Najera, Ivan
Nakatake, Hiroko
Nalezyty, Dennis
Napier, Joe
Nash, Jamie
Nasr, Sima
Nathan, Lauren
Neault, Michael
Nedorostek, Nathan
Neely, Jeffrey
Neff, Paula
Nehring, Sike
Nelson, Brian
Nemecek, Sasha
Neulieb, Zac
Neumann, Ini
Ng, Edmond
Nguyen Phu, Hai
Nguyen, Alex
Nguyen, Dang
Nguyen, Hai
Nguyen, Michele-Hoaiduc
Nicklos, Gus

Nicolas, Benjamin
Nishimoto, John
Niu, Max
Nneji, Amana
Noble, Steve
Noble, Steven
Norris, James
O'Brien, Nick
O'Casey, Kade
O'Hara, David
O'Hara, Keeley
O'Neil, DJ
Obrist, Jessica
Ogawa, Masahiro
Ogilvie, Shane
Oguma, Chikako
Ohanessian, Shadia
Olsen, Louise
Oltman, Brandon
Ordonez, Cristian
Oreamuno, Ignacio
Ormandy, Stephen
Oros, Michelle
Ortiz, Cruz
Ownbey, Dan
Oyamada, Iku
Palmbäck, Thomas
Pantuso, Michael
Papa, Andrew
Paprocki, Greg
Paramski, Scott
Parkerson, Bailey
Patterson, Pam
Paul, Nicholas
Peña, Fidel
Peng, Yutien
Penning, Steve
PepsiCo Design & Innovation
Peraza, Deroy
Perez, Alvaro
Perez, Miguel
Perry, Alvin
Perry, Nate
Peschel, Dan
Petersen, Jon
Petersen, Scott
Peterson, Hannah
Petrina, Joe
Pettus, Tom
Peutzer, Zach
Pfeffer, Stefanie
Pfeifer, Erich
Phillips, Joshua
Phillips, Max
Piecha, John
Pinfold, Myles
Pishnery, Keith
Plazonja, Jonathan
Plioplis, Marcelo
Plourde Khoury, Melissa
Podlogar, Chelsea
Poelker, Diane
Pohlman, Jenny
Poirier, Jordan
Poole, Dean
Portnoy, Oleg
Potton, Niko
Poulin, Richard
Pratt, Guy
Pratt, Rob

Presiado, Arnie
Preston, Lilly
Pridgen, Scott
Prihoda, Nick
Principe, Paul
Proffit, Tony
Psimaris, Konstantinos
Purtilar, Chet
Putri, Rika
Pylypczak, John
Que, Lan
Queirós, António
Quinn, Brendan
Quinones, Reece
Quinton, Greg
Radford, Stuart
Rahav, Amnon
Raine, Johnlee
Rakatansky, Charlie
Ramirez-Hunt, Emi
Ramirez, Karla
Ramos, Alfonso
Ramos, Janie
Ramos, Jose
Rankine, Justine
Rao, Vijoy
Redding, Tika
Rei, Raquel
Reile, Emily
Reilly, Rob
Remillard-Larose, Eve
Remphrey, Matthew
Renac, Angela
Renfro, Kurt
Reynolds, Mark
Rhodes, Anthony P.
Rillo, Derek
Rimon, Orly
Risch, Kayla
Robak, Kim
Roberts, Dave
Robertson, Jill
Roche, Julie
Rockow, Carol
Rodick, Peter
Rodman, Neil
Rodriguez, Ramon
Roizin, Or
Roka, Alex
Roman, Peter
Romanelli, Andrea
Rosati, Martina
Rossi, Pete
Rossignol, Jen
Rothermich, J. Kenneth
Rothman, Jason
Rouette, Andrée
Roumieu, Graham
Roy, Susan
Rubino, Regina
Rudd, Olly
Rugari, Christian
Russack, Evan
Ruth, Jeff
Rutherford, Emma
Ryan, Vanessa
Saavedra, Cindy
Sabach, Jan
Sabatino, Mike
Sack, Ron
Sade, Ayelet

Safar, Studio
Sagmeister, Stefan
Salyer, Andre
Samuel, Derek
San Miguel, David
Sano, Yusuke
Santiesban, Eduardo
Sardesai, Amol
Sasges, Rita
Saulino, Amanda
Savage, Gail
Savasky, Julie
Scales, Libby
Schachterle, Jim
Schaeffer, George
Scharpf, Tom
Schatz, Howard
Schelhas, Hans
Schierhout, Megan
Schmidt, Anders
Schmidt, Julie
Schneider, Deborah
Schneider, Todd
Schnepf, Michael
Schroeder, Sarah
Schuler, Natalie
Schulte, Jason
Schulz, Christian R.
Schulz, Hanna
Schwab, Michael
Schwabacher, Martin
Schwartz, Mark
Schwarz, David
Scommegna, Roger
Scott, Aaron
Scott, Laura
Scragg, Mark
Scuderi, Jason
Seager, Daniel
Seimetz-Duncan, Diane
Seitz, Theresa
Sera Garcia, Anna
Sfetko, Jason
Shamlian, Fred
Shaw, Kevin
Sheeler, Jen
Shim, Kyuha
Shimada, Maho
Shimizu, Kayoko
Shoan, Tatijana
Shoji, Sayuri
Silveira, Jeferson
Silverstein, Sheralyn
Sim, Junhee
Sim, Kay
Simões, Ana
Simpson, Taylor
Skinner, Phil
Slusher, Rick
Smart, Andrew
Smith, Alan
Smith, Andrew
Smith, Brian E.
Smith, Buck
Smith, Heather Christian
Smith, Jaclyn
Smith, Jake
Smith, Lindsey
Smith, Mike
Smith, Pat
Smolover, Charles

Smolover, Charlie
Smrczek, Ron
Snyder, James
Solanet, Mathilde
Solly, Vanessa
Soloduha, Natalia
Sommerhuber, Lisa
South, Michelle
Spacher, Alexander
Spassov, Petre
Spencer, Kate
Spiller, Jennie
Spitzley, Gale
Sposato, John
Spreafico, Martino
Stark, Veronica
Steele, Brian
Steichen, Kyle
Steinhardt, Nick
Steinke, Dave
Stember-Richards, Diane
Sterling, Jennifer
Stern, Heather
Stevens, Brad
Stevens, Clover
Stewart, Charles
Stoik, Ted
Stojanovic, Slavimir
Stout, DJ
Strandell, Strom
Strange, James
Sturgeon, Pete
Sullivan, Thomas
Suminski, Ken
Sungkar, Jefton
Surace, Cosimo
Swingle, Juli
Sych, Paul
Tai, Eugenia
Takamoto, Akihiro
Takayama, Steve
Takimoto, Kei
Talbot, Jenn
Talbot, Jennifer
Talbott, Megan
Talford, Paula
Tan, Heidi
Taylor, John
Taylor, Matt
Taylor, Steven
Taylor, Stu
Taylor, William
Teiga, Xose
Temple, Sean
Templeton, Campbell
Teo, Sunny
Terpening, Lori
Terwilliger, Jodi
Test, Katie
Tetsill, Jamie Bruski
Tevere, Virginia
The, Cassia
Théophane, Clare
Thoelke, Eric
Thomas, Chris
Thomas, Greg
Thomas, Steven
Thompson, David
Thornlow, Alexis
Thrasher, Christy
Tilford, Jeff

Tobin, E. Patrick
Tomita, Hideaki
Tomkins, Dan
Tomlinson, Darwin
Toms, Stuart
Toro, Alyssa
Torrance, Kate
Torres, Rosangel
Tracy Padilla, Talbott
Tremblay, Frédéric
Trickel, Sue
Trickel, Susan
Trueblood, Peter
Tsao, Hsin-chi
Tu, Emily
Tubkam, Ithinand
Tuncay, Haluk
Turner, David
Tutssel, Glenn
Uhlein, Thomas
Vakser Zeltser, Julia
Valdez, Julie
Valdis, Unnur
Varini, Felice
Varming, Søren
Vaschetto, Anne
Vasquez, Ramon
Vawter, David
Vecerka, Albert
Vellozzi, Eric
Venables, Paul
Venn, Glenda
Ventimiglia, Tim
Vermeulen, Aleisha
Vermeulen, Chandra
Victor, Novak
Vieira, Paula
Vlack, Alex
Vollmöller, Bernd
Vwater, David
Wadekar, Akshata
Waggoner, Brady
Wagner, Jamey
Wahlgren, Lina
Wainwright, Karen
Wajdowicz, Jurek
Walczak, Shari
Walker, Simon
Wall, Hayley
Waller, Alexis
Walls, Jim
Walsh, Jessica
Walsh, Joe
Walsh, Michael J.
Walter, Tammo
Walters, Lee
Wang, Angie
Wang, Annie
Ward Hill, Jessica
Ward, Trish
Washington, Melissa
Watanabe, Hitomi
Waters, Mark
Watson, Mark "Monkey"
Watts, Peter
Weber, Noelle
Webster, Dave
Weeks, Ben
Weese, Catharine
Weis, Annika
Weiss, Chad

Weiss, Jo Maitland
Weitz, Carter
Wells, Brandon
Wells, Justin
Wessel, Kyle
West, Kerina
Wheeler, Benjamin
White, Roy
Whiteley, Alastair
Whitman, Robert
Whittington, Ty
Wiesner, Nick
Wightman, Jodie
Williams, Clay
Williams, Trevor
Wilson, Barbara
Wilson, Dean
Winburn, Jane
Windham, Courtney
Winkler, Marissa
Winn, Jonathan
Wiser, Soung
Witteck, Patrick
Wojciechowski, Christian
Wolf, Karl
Wolf, Piera
Wolfgramm, Alan
Wolfson, Alisa
Womack, Andrew
Wong, Genevieve
Wong, Raymond
Wong, Tracy
Wood, Greg
Wood, Ryan
Woodward, Fred
Woodward, Sherryl
Wozniak, David
Wragg, Carlin
Wreland, Markus
Wright, Claire
Wright, Kris
Wright, Laura Belle
Wylie, Sean
Wyllie, Lauren
Wymond, Greer
Xavier, Roger
Xi, Xiaohui
Yamashita, Ricky
Yang, Erik
Yarbrough, Adam
Yeaton, Tom
Yetter, Jim
Yoo, Chung
Yoshida-Carrera, Yoko
Yuen, Amy
Yuen, Kin
Yule, Jonathan
Yule, Jonathon
Zafra, Marta
Zalla, Mary
Zambarbieri, Orlando
Zavacky, Michael
Zeilinger, Allison
Zettler, Jessie
Zhao, Miao

Congratulations to all the entrants!

See your entry archived at graphis.com with a full-screen presentation.

You can upgrade your status, filtering your respective Country, State or Province.

Poster Annual 2015

GraphisPosterAnnual2015

PLATINUM WINNERS:

Fons Hickmann
Hajime Tsushima
Dean Poole
Geray Gencer
Michael Vanderbyl
Scott Laserow
Jan Sabach
Kuokwai Cheong
Nanette Bercu

2014
Hardcover: 240 pages
200-plus color illustrations

Trim: 8.5 x 11.75"
ISBN: 978-1-932026-89-4
US $120

This book is a collection of the year's best work from some of the world's top poster designers. We start by featuring a commentary with Bettina Richter, curator at the Museum für Gestaltung in Zürich, who oversees the management and selection of the most extensive poster collection in Switzerland. Medalists include **João Machado, Fons Hickmann, Toshiaki & Hisa Ide, Sarah Castelblanco, Danny Warner, Stephan Bundi, Melissa Baillache, Chikako Oguma, Skolos-Wedell, Toyotsugu Itoh, Michael Vanderbyl** and **Raymond Tam**, among many others. Each winner receives a full-page presentation of their work, along with a list of all the entrants. Up to 900 submissions were received and a majority of this work will be archived permanently on our website, all receiving an equal presentation.

Advertising Annual 2014

GraphisAdvertisingAnnual2014

Advertising is really problem solving, and when you do it in a really creative way, it's art. Jera Mehrdad, *M.D. Saatchi & Saatchi, LA*

2014
Hardcover: 240 pages
200-plus color illustrations

Trim: 8.5 x 11.75"
ISBN: 978-1932026-86-3
US $120

This book presents some of the top campaigns of the year, selected from hundreds of entries. Featured are seasoned works from accomplished advertising agencies such as award winners **3e The Life Time Agency, BRIGHT RED\TBWA, Butler, Shine, Stern & Partners, LLOYD&CO, PP+K, Publicis Kaplan Thaler, The Richards Group, Zulu Alpha Kilo, Goodby Silverstein & Partners, 160over90** and **Saatchi & Saatchi, LA**. Each ad is presented on a full page with a case study describing the Assignment: along with an in-depth description on the solution and the result. This provides insight into the agency's creative process and how they met the needs of their clients. The Graphis Platinum, Gold and Silver winning entries are an essential reference for advertising professionals, clients and students.

Design Annual 2014

GraphisDesignAnnual2014

PLATINUM WINNERS:

Lorenc+Yoo Design
Vanderbyl Design
Dankook University
IF Studio
SDG/Inne Design
Pentagram
Stranger&Stranger
Sandstrom Partners

2014
Hardcover: 256 pages
200-plus color illustrations

Trim: 8.5 x 11.75"
ISBN: 978-1-932026-85-6
US $120

Graphis Design Annual 2014 is the eminent international showcase of premiere work produced in all areas of contemporary graphic design. Featuring full-page layouts of the best in creative excellence and innovation, this book covers categories that include annual reports, branding, posters, books, catalogues, music, CDs, Exhibits, Packaging and more. In these pages you will find Q&As with **Andrea Castelletti, Sandstrom Partners, Studio Hinrichs, Thirst, Webster, omdr Co., Ltd., Lorenc+Yoo Design Inc., Andrea Castelletti, Designory, GQ, Frost* Design Sydney** and **Vanderbyl Design,** in addition to companies listed on the cover of the book. Also included is a complete credits and commentary that delves deep into each work. The result is an indispensable resource for all design professionals and their clients.

Photography Annual 2014

2014
Hardcover: 256 pages
200-plus color illustrations

Trim: 8.5 x 11.75"
ISBN: 978-1-932026-87-0
US $120

This book features an interview with photographer Caroline Knopf, a former stylist with great taste, discussing her transition to photography and the fine art-based influences behind her work. This year, Graphis awarded 11 Platinums, 54 Golds and 64 Silvers, totaling 129 medalists. Close to 300 submissions in this book will be archived permanently on our website, which can be further accessed by Region or Country, State or Province. This will bring everyone included a continued rise in the hierarchy of the show. We present winners with a full-page presentation and Credits and Commentary in the book as well as on the website. Medalists include **Henry Leutwyler, Mark Stetler, Sandro, Phil Marco, Kristofer Dan-Bergman, Tatijana Shoan, Raymundo Garza, Laurie Frankel** and **Parish Kohanim**.

New Talent Annual 2014

GraphisNewTalentAnnual2014

Creative talent is powerful. Powerful enough to make us laugh, cry, think. If you don't believe us, throw this book at someone's face and see how powerful great talent can be. Jay Maisel & Alexis Beltrone a.k.a JayLex, *Freshmen*

2014
Hardcover: 256 pages
200-plus color illustrations

Trim: 7 x 11.75"
ISBN: 978-1-932026-88-7
US $120

This book is a collection of the year's best work from Professors who have managed to demand and inspire brilliance from their students. Most of this work matches the caliber of top professionals in the industry. In this year's edition, we feature commentary from the students of the eight platinum-winning instructors: **Phil Bekker, Bill Oberlander, Paul Sahre, Louise Fili, Nic Taylor, Piotr Kunce, Carin Goldberg** and **Behnoush McKay**. Graphis also awarded 48 Golds and 54 Silvers and 64 Merits, totaling 174 medalists. This book presents winning work with full-page presentations, along with a list of all entrants. Up to 900 submissions to this book will be archived permanently on our website, all work receives an equal presentation on our site.

Branding 6

GraphisBranding6

8 EXCEPTIONAL BRANDING CASE STUDIES:

Pentagram
WAX
People Design
Cue
Firewood Inc.
The General Design
Studio International
Alt Group

2013
Hardcover: 256 pages
200-plus color illustrations

Trim: 8.5 x 11.75"
ISBN: 1-932026-78-8
US $120

This book presents interviews, company profiles and visual histories of some of the biggest names in design and retail today, including: Q&A with **Pentagram, WAX, People design, Cue, Firewood, The General Design Co., Studio International, Alt Group, The General Design Co., DNA Design, Decker Design, Inc., Concrete Design Communications, Landor Associates, Ameba Design Ltd., Claus Koch, Concrete Design Communications, Cue, DDB Canada, Ellen Bruss Design, LLC., Firewood, Higher, Mark Oliver, Inc.** and **TOKY Branding + Design.** All that, plus multiple images from the year's Graphis Gold Award-winning branding campaigns. This is a must-have for anyone interested in successful, creative branding — designers, businesses, students and fans alike.

You can view all entries at www. Graphis .com

The majority of entries are permanently archived at www.Graphis.com.
Anyone can upgrade their status by filtering Country, State or Province.